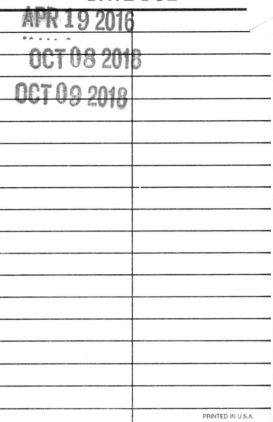

MW00993310

To discover new countries,
to climb the highest peaks,
to travel through new areas of celestial space,
to turn our searchlights
upon domains of eternal darkness,
that is what makes life worth living.
—AUGUSTE PICCARD

Tianfei, the Chinese goddess of sailors and seafarers

LIVES OF THE EXPLORERS

Discoveries, Disasters
(and What the Neighbors Thought)

WRITTEN BY **Kathleen Krull**

ILLUSTRATED BY **Kathryn Hewitt**

Houghton Mifflin Harcourt
Boston New York

Welcome to Cassius and Julius, current and future explorers.

—K.K.

To Steve and Yong

("Man was born with legs, not roots." —R. Buckminster Fuller)

—K.H.

CONTENTS

LIVES OF THE EXPLORERS

INTRODUCTION

Exploring the unknown: it's what humans do. Since the beginning of time, we have wanted to know what else might be out there.

Though many explorers are lost to history, we know some by name. Here, presented chronologically, are the biographies of twenty bright stars of geography. Other books trace the east-west-north-south details of their journeys to faraway countries (referred to here by their present-day names, though they might have been called something else in the past). This book is about the explorers as human beings—warts, egos, and all. Some were not well-liked by their neighbors or anyone else; many were cruel. But all were bold and determined. These were men and women who took a deep breath, got up out of their chairs, and went adventuring by land, sea, or air.

Their motives varied. Many were lured by glamour and the possibility of riches. Others were driven by curiosity or a passion for expanding human knowledge about the world. Still others wanted to escape the boredom of their settled lives. The journey of a heroic explorer—especially if he or she was a good writer, which many of these were—often inspired others to get moving.

The stress of facing the unknown day after day is not for the faint of heart.

Homesickness was the least of an explorer's problems. Who had to follow a path of bones—human and animal—across the sands of the "Sea of Death"? (Polo.) Whose cat screamed across the deck, warning of disaster? (Hudson's.) Which explorer had a young crew of more than 250, of whom only eighteen made it home? (Magellan.) Who lost eleven of his crew to cannibals? (Cook.) Who was accidentally shot by one of his own men? (Lewis.) Who emerged from a swamp covered in black slime and leeches, weak from loss of blood? (Kingsley.) Which ones got totally lost? (Columbus—and many others.) Who survived kidnapping? (Battuta and Boone.) Who was taunted, spat at, stoned, and had people try to break down her door? (Bird.)

And some explorers failed to survive at all. Their trips were life-or-death journeys with every possible danger, few conveniences, and no GPS.

Many of the courageous people here were inspired by books about explorers that they'd read in childhood. May this book inspire you to also forge new paths, remaining brave and full of wonder even when everything ahead of you is unknown.

—Kathleen Krull

LIVES OF THE EXPLORERS

IN SEARCH OF TREES

LEIF ERICSON

BORN IN ICELAND(?), 970(?)
DIED IN GREENLAND(?), 1020(?)

Viking famed as the first European to set foot in North America

Even baby Vikings knew their way around a boat, and Leif Ericson knew more than most. He grew up on a cliff overlooking the ocean, in a house made of mud and stone. His dad, Eric the Red, had come from Scandinavia and discovered Greenland, and the family settled in one of its nicer areas. But the winters seemed endless, and there were no trees—no green (ironically), no shade, no timber for building houses.

Ericson grew up hearing magical tales of lands covered with forests. At about age twenty-one, taking along some thirty others, he set out to find them.

In sagas told around the fire for the next ten centuries, Ericson was "a large, strong man, of very striking appearance and wise, as well as being a man of moderation in all things." Vikings in general were more famous for fierceness than moderation. They carried weapons at all times (axes, swords, arrows, spears), wore shirts made of bearskin, and howled like wolves to frighten their enemies.

Aboard ship, Ericson's men ate fresh whale, seal, or caribou. At night they passed the time with stories about Thor and other gods. They played a game similar to chess; they carved spoons or figurines of gods from wood or bone. They doubled up to sleep in the animal-skin sacks that they used for holding tools.

Ericson landed in North America very pleased indeed: temperatures were above freezing, huge salmon jumped out of the rivers, the green grass would feed the livestock, and the landscape was dense with trees. He spent the winter and then sailed home, his boat loaded with precious timber.

His voyage inspired other explorers, while Ericson stayed in Greenland as the master of his estate. When he died at about age fifty, he left it all to his son.

Almost everything known about Leif Ericson was guesswork until 1961. In Newfoundland, on the coast of Canada, archaeologists found the remains of an ancient Greenland-style settlement, complete with a woodworking shop—believed to be Ericson's.

"Only the Half of What I Saw"
Marco Polo

Born in 1254(?) and Died in 1324 in Venice, Italy

Italian who was the first European to explore China

Marco Polo's father was a merchant, the job everyone in Venice wanted. One successful trip to a faraway place for rare goods could make a family permanently wealthy. In highest demand were jewels, spices, Turkish carpets, and especially silk. Silk was so precious because it was rare, made only in China by women who took the strands that silkworms produced and transformed them into gorgeous cloth.

Polo's dad was away so long on a trading trip that Marco was fifteen before they met. Having grown up with relatives after his mother died, the boy had assumed he was an orphan. When his father and uncle invited him to join their next trip, he jumped at the chance. The older Polos had promised to bring holy oil from Jerusalem to Kubla Khan, emperor of China, and do a lot of trading on the way.

The three planned to sail, but when they saw their shoddy ships—held together with coconut twine, not nails—they quickly changed their plans and set off on what was later known as the Silk Road. This ancient system of trails, thousands of miles long, was the only known route into China by land.

Every morning, they would leave behind their fires (made with camel poo) and take off in the chilly hour before sunrise. When all went well, the Polos could cover twenty miles a day.

Each of those days brought an adventure. They frolicked with hundreds of wild sheep that had curly horns measuring five feet. They sipped a soup of Russian olives, Chinese cabbage, and the sliced thorax of a sheep. They visited people in a pearl-rich area who wore little except pearls, and Buddhist monasteries full of thousands of devout monks wearing scratchy sacks of blue and black. They met Mongolians who had trained themselves to go for days without eating, drinking the blood of their precious horses to keep from starving. They winced at men and women covered from head to toe with ornate tattoos, which at the time was such a painful and bloody process that it could be fatal.

Luckily, Marco kept a journal. At first he felt superior to cultures other than his own, but as the months passed, he grew more open-minded. He took a special interest in Buddhism, though he always presented himself as a devout Christian. Actually, he became expert at blending in wherever he was, like a chameleon.

The trail took the Polos through some of the most hostile places on the planet. One mountainous region was known as the "roof of the world" because the air was so thin that even birds didn't go there. They narrowly escaped bandits intent on kidnapping them and selling them as slaves. They evaded Indian pirates who would have forced them to drink seawater with tamarind until they vomited, in order to search for gems that could have been swallowed.

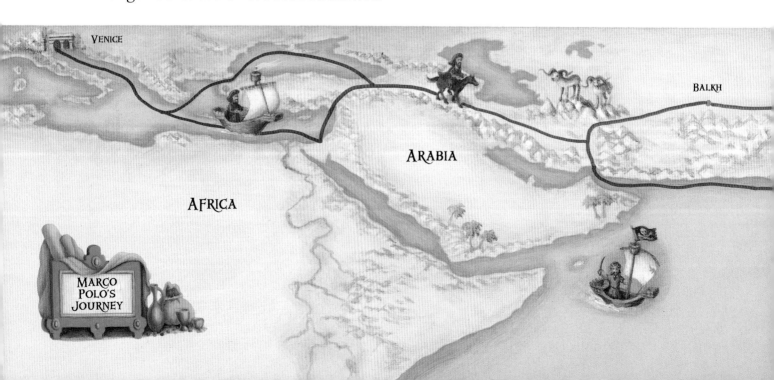

VENICE

BALKH

ARABIA

AFRICA

MARCO POLO'S JOURNEY

Marco did fall ill, possibly with tuberculosis. The Polos spent a year in a beautiful area now known as Afghanistan so he could recover in the clean, pure air, perhaps aided by the local opium. Marco was aghast at the nearby ruins of Balkh. Once a great metropolis, it was known as the Screaming City because it had been reduced to rubble by Genghis Khan's warriors, who had killed every inhabitant.

The last part of the journey took them across the "Sea of Death" desert. Riding at night because the days were just too hot, they followed a path marked by piles of bones—some animal, some human. The sands, notorious as the "Singing Sands," seemed to howl at them in the creepiest way.

At last, after three years and eight thousand miles, they reached their goal: China and the welcoming court of Emperor Kubla Khan. This Khan, grandson of Genghis, ruled the largest empire in the world.

Marco thought the Khan was simply over-the-top, sitting on his throne wearing robes of pure gold, a tame lion curled up at his feet. He had ten thousand white horses and about one hundred children. At his gigantic parties, complete with amusing performers of all kinds, elephants would stream in bearing gifts from his subjects.

The Polos were treated like royalty—the Khan wanted them to say good things about him when they got home. They didn't really have a choice about how to spend their time; one didn't say no to the Khan. He gave twenty-year-old Marco the job of

traveling all over the empire to gather gossip, carrying a golden tablet that ordered everyone to treat him well. Still blending in wherever he was, Marco spoke Persian and various Mongol dialects, though he never learned Chinese.

Everything about China blew Marco away and was recorded in his journals. In Beijing, the impressive capital, thousands of carriages brought in precious raw silk every day. The city of Hangzhou, the largest in the world at that time, was lovely and well-organized, with citizens reading books and eating steamed pancakes in tiny cafés. Marco learned that those strange black burning rocks were coal, meaning he could heat water for a hot bath every day (a bizarre notion to Venetians, who rarely bathed). He saw private indoor bathrooms (unlike in Venice, where chamber pots got dumped out the window). He gasped at hideously large snakes that turned out to be crocodiles, and other creatures he claimed were unicorns, but were Asian rhinoceroses. He heard the loudest sound he'd ever heard: the blast of gunpowder, then unknown in Europe.

Fourteen years went by. The Polos begged the Khan to let them return home, but he enjoyed their company—and having them around made him feel powerful. Finally he gave them a job that allowed them to sail away: escorting a woman known as the Blue Princess to her wedding in Iran, leaving them free to continue on to Venice. The whole journey home took the Venetians three years, and only eighteen of the original crew of six hundred survived it. Dreadful things happened to them, but Marco's journals are mysteriously mute about the details.

When the Polos limped into Venice, filthy and ragged after their journey, the other Polos didn't recognize them. Then the men ripped open their robes to reveal a fortune in jewels, making for a happy reunion. When Marco started blabbing all the things he'd seen, he was nicknamed "Marco Millions" by those who thought he was telling millions of lies. He had been to places no European had seen, and some simply didn't believe his tales.

Was Marco, now forty-one, bored by his old life on land? Or was he irritated by the children taunting "Mister Marco, tell us another lie"? Perhaps, because he didn't settle down; he commanded a boat during a war between Venice and Genoa. He was captured and spent a year in a Genoese prison. It wasn't too bad—he had a comfortable apartment, possibly even servants. He was able to send for his journals, and with the help of a fellow prisoner wrote a book about his adventures: *The Travels of Marco Polo.*

He married at forty-five; had three daughters, named Fantina, Bellela, and Moreta; and bought a palazzo in a stylish neighborhood. For the rest of his life, until he died at age sixty-nine, Marco Polo worked as a merchant and told his stories to anyone who would listen. He never left Venice again.

"I have only told the half of what I saw" was his refrain.

ONWARD

⁓ Polo's trustworthiness wasn't questioned just by his fellow Venetians. Most scholars today detect some exaggerations in his book, though deem it basically true. One person who never doubted was Christopher Columbus, who had a much-thumbed, notated copy of *Travels* with him on his boat in 1492 as he looked for a sea route to places Polo described.

⁓ Polo's greatest contribution to geography may have been inspiring increasingly accurate maps. He didn't draw maps himself, but by using his rough measurement of "a day's journey," others were able to.

⁓ The children's game Marco Polo, a form of tag played in water, is named for him, though no one is sure when or where the game started. One player calls out "Marco!" in an attempt to locate and tag other players, who yell back "Polo!" (Of course, if Marco himself were playing, he'd call out "Me! Me!")

KINDNESS OF STRANGERS

IBN BATTUTA

BORN IN 1304 AND DIED IN 1368(?) IN TANGIER, MOROCCO

Muslim explorer from North Africa who traveled 75,000 miles in thirty years

The most-miles-traveled award, at least for the medieval era, goes to Ibn Battuta. A devout Sunni Muslim, he set out from Morocco at age twenty-two to make the traditional pilgrimage to Mecca, several thousand miles away—and just kept going.

His life as a religious scholar and judge in Tangier had been comfortable. Well-educated, he could pepper his conversations with poetry, Koran quotes, and references to classic Arabic literature. He dressed like a legal scholar, in a large turban and a spotless gown of fine fabric.

Battuta's travels as a poor holy man were not always so comfy. He explored much of Arabia, then India, Southeast Asia, Spain, and parts of Africa, always with the goal of finding the holiest people there. Sometimes he thought of staying to study with them, and sometimes he cried from homesickness, especially when he learned from far away of the death of his father, then a son, and then his mother. But he was too restless, too curious, to stop exploring. "Never take the same road twice" was his motto.

Unable to swim and uncomfortable around water, Battuta preferred traveling on land. He was treated generously at Christian monasteries and at way stations that took care of Muslim holy men. Sometimes he joined caravans for companionship.

Other times he was helped by kind local rulers who might give him clean clothes with coins sewed into them, as well as horses and slaves for his journey.

Battuta frowned on those who smoked hashish, drank alcohol, or neglected their prayers. He hated markets that stank of rotten fruit, too much fresh fish, and the blood of slaughtered camels flowing in the street—all common at the time. Men in bathhouses without towels around their waists bothered him, as did women whose heads weren't covered or who had male friends, all of which he considered immodest. He despised violence toward others—slaves being abused, or the practice of forcing criminals to eat human excrement.

He blended in and felt at home almost everywhere, except China. He found everything there to be foreign to him, which "distressed me so much that I stayed at home and went out only when it was necessary."

A fan of the spiritual and physical beauty of women, Battuta married at least ten times and fathered at least five children. He rarely took the wives or children traveling with him—the women's families objected. Six of the marriages took place on the heavenly Maldive Islands, after Battuta got over his horror at the skimpy islander outfits: "When I was a religious judge there, I tried to put an end to this practice and ordered them to wear clothes, but I met with no success."

Death threatened Battuta at every turn. Once he was so ill with a high fever that he tied himself to his horse's saddle so he wouldn't fall. Hot winds could dry up every source of water; the price of a mouthful reached enormous sums. Deathly cold would force him to wear so many bulky layers that he had to be lifted onto his horse. In a pirate attack he lost everything except for a single pair of pants, and in a bandit attack he was wounded by arrows.

But he also met with extraordinary hospitality. Once when he was lost for days without food or drink, his feet swollen and bleeding, a stranger approached and carried Battuta on his back to shelter. He seldom went hungry. A simple meal would be bread, cheese, olives, fresh dates. He enjoyed melons, white apricots, coconuts, anything sweetened with sugar or carob, and a kind of lizard with its insides replaced with turmeric.

After thirty years Battuta returned for good to Morocco, deciding it was "the best of countries," though it was one of the few places he had never explored.

When the Sultan commanded him to record his memories, Battuta produced a vivid account. Centuries later, it reached Europe, revealing a wealth of information about large parts of the Muslim world, enlarging everyone's horizons.

Today, if you travel to Dubai, a city on the Arabian Peninsula, you can visit the gigantic Ibn Battuta Mall, named for this most famous of Arabic explorers.

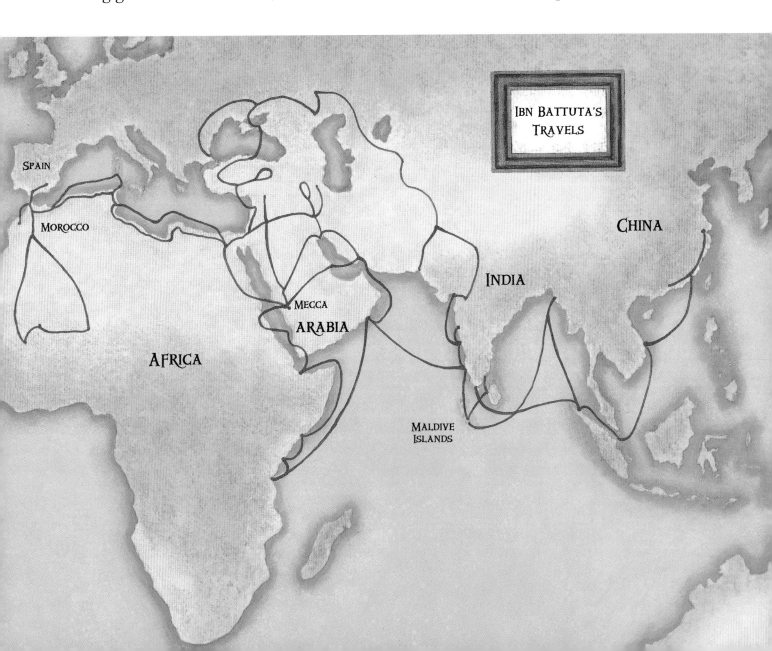

Everyone Likes Presents

Zheng He

Born in Yunnan Province, China, 1371(?)
Died in Calicut, India, 1433

Chinese commander of seven voyages to thirty countries

It was good to be trusted by the emperor Yongle, who tended to execute any-one who challenged him. No one was more reliable than Zheng He. He had lived in the emperor's household since he was ten, when he had been captured by generals of the Ming dynasty of China, the richest and most populated country on earth.

Zheng became trusted both inside the palace (he rose to director of the palace servants, which entitled him to wear robes of red, not blue like the others) and out-side the palace, as a courageous officer in the army.

Some say he was seven feet tall, with a waist five feet around. He had a voice like a gong, rough skin like an orange peel, and a powerful gaze with eyebrows like swords. He grew up a devout Muslim, later became a devout Buddhist, and also worshiped the Taoist sea goddess Tianfei, protector of sailors against the giant drag-ons believed to live under the surface.

Finally the emperor rewarded the thirty-five-year-old Zheng with a plum job: commander in chief of a most unusual voyage, bearing gifts and gathering informa-tion in Asia, India, Arabia, and Africa. Chinese scholars gave Zheng the latest Arab and Hindu discoveries about navigation and geography.

No expense was spared for his fleet of sixty ships. They may have been the biggest wooden boats ever built—huge "treasure ships" (filled with the gifts) guarded by smaller ones. A complex system of flags, lanterns, gongs, drums, and carrier pigeons enabled the ships to communicate with one another.

Zheng's crew was massive—about thirty thousand men, mostly professional soldiers, living in comfortable quarters. Also aboard were 180 doctors to collect medicinal herbs wherever they went; judges to settle disputes and punish those who broke rules; translators; farmers to grow vegetables and keep everyone healthy; and one officer whose only duty was to tell fortunes.

The countries Zheng visited got the finest silks and brocades with dragon and phoenix designs, paper money, and more. Countries also sent back their own presents, such as pepper, worth its weight in gold, and animals unknown in China: ostriches, zebras, camels, Arabian horses. Elegant giraffes caused the biggest sensation.

Zheng and his men were showered with money and promotions when they returned to China. The emperor hosted banquets in their honor, with more food and drink than was humanly possible to consume.

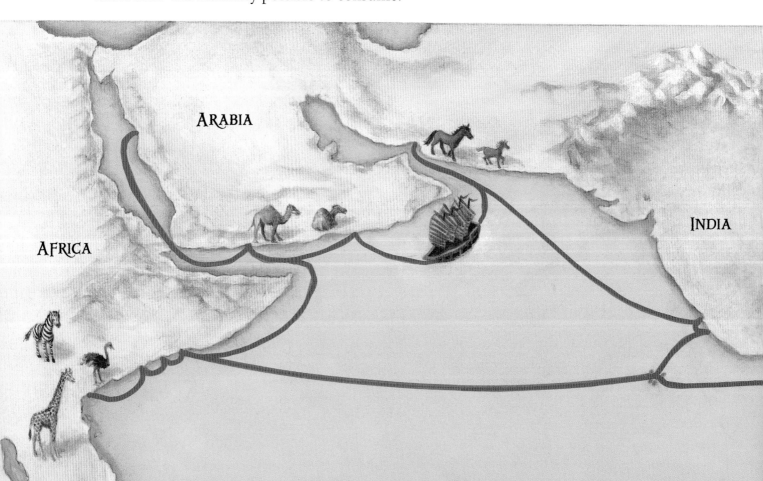

Zheng took a total of seven voyages, the goal always to inspire awe at Chinese accomplishments. He was not out to conquer; his ships had names like *Lasting Tranquility* and *Pure Harmony*. They were fully armed with guns, explosives, grenades, bows, and flaming arrows, but Zheng preferred to avoid trouble and used force only three times in order to repel attacks.

Zheng did have enemies: officials who deemed the extravagant voyages in bad taste and a waste of resources. They accused him of lying about what he saw, lies that ordinary citizens couldn't prove one way or the other.

Zheng ultimately owned a huge house near the main mosque in Nanjing, with seventy-two rooms and lots of land. When he died at age sixty-two and was buried at sea, all of it went to his adopted nephew.

Had the voyages continued, the world might look very different today due to China's influence. But Emperor Yongle had also died. The records of Zheng's voyages were "lost," the treasure ships rotted, and China withdrew from the sea and stopped exploring.

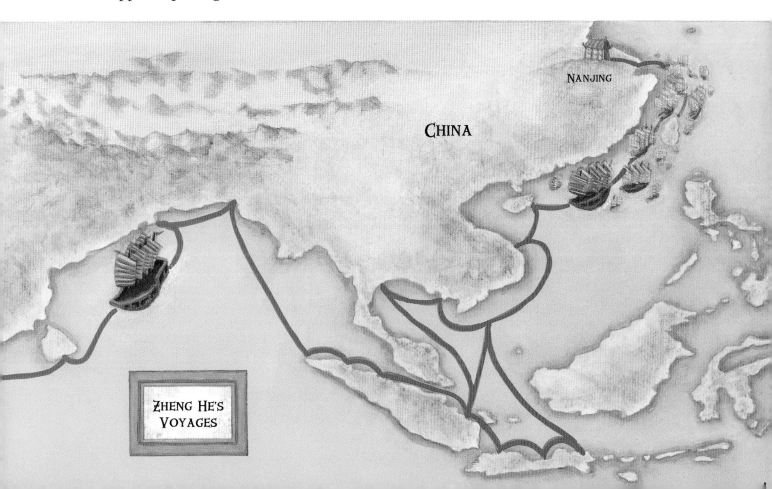

NANJING

CHINA

ZHENG HE'S VOYAGES

"Gold Is Most Excellent"

Christopher Columbus

Born in Genoa, Italy, 1451
Died in Valladolid, Spain, 1506

Italian commander who brought the Americas to Europe's attention

It had been weeks since they'd last seen land. Most sailors in the 1400s were deeply superstitious and couldn't stand the idea of not staying within view of a shore. Anything could happen as they crossed the Sea of Darkness, defenseless. Would magnetic forces suck them under? Would sea monsters rise up and swallow entire ships? Would the sea start to boil, or would it turn too thick for them to move?

And if they did reach land, would they find humans? Or monsters with tails, eyes in their shoulders, umbrella feet, or the heads of dogs? What about cannibals eager to eat them, or fierce women who lived alone and killed any man they saw?

The men were all sleep-deprived from their routine of four hours on duty, four hours of rest. The areas for sleeping were uncomfortable and smelly, with fleas, rats, and lice everywhere. Sailors were irritated, bored, and very nervous.

Perhaps the only person on this voyage who was unafraid was their captain, Christopher Columbus. At forty-one, his once-red hair now gray, he wore a red silk jacket, had a red face, and was not particularly popular. He didn't care—this journey was his dream come true.

Columbus had been proving his bravery all his life. He claimed to have gone to sea at the age of ten, leaving behind his father, a wool merchant. In his twenties he survived a shipwreck off Portugal, floating on an oar and swimming six miles to shore. Never mind that he was wounded.

He returned to sea on missions to various countries, learning everything he could about navigation and studying every available map. He liked to take along his sons: Diego (whose mother was the daughter of a nobleman) and Ferdinand (whose mother was a peasant). Not formally educated, he read whatever he could; *The Travels of Marco Polo* was a favorite. In all of his books he underlined every reference to gold two or three times, and his "Grand Scheme" was to find gold by sailing to Asia, specifically the East Indies.

Columbus had spent the last eight years asking in vain for money from Portugal, Italy, and England so he could fund the voyage. His personality didn't seem to help his quest. A Portuguese court historian called him "a big talker and boastful." He once beat up a representative of a bishop he needed on his side. Nor did his demands help: he insisted on the title of "Great Admiral of the Ocean," being appointed governor of all lands he discovered, and receiving one-tenth of all income.

Spain finally agreed to fund his risky trip, not fully expecting him to return. But Queen Isabella was a passionate Catholic (she had just "cleansed" Spain of Jews and Muslims), and she was intrigued by the idea of claiming new countries to convert. Columbus was just as religious, so devout that one son said he never swore (unusual for a sailor) except to say "By San Fernando!"

Now he was in charge of the *Niña*, the *Pinta*, and the *Santa María*, three small ships manned by ninety Spaniards, sailing off any known map. Technically, Columbus was lost—but he was also lucky. The sea stayed calm, so did his men, and on October 12, 1492, five weeks after they started, they reached the Bahama island of San Salvador, also called Watlings Island.

Columbus couldn't wait to jump ashore and find the gold. He planted a flag to claim the area for Spain, unaware at first that people had been living on the island for thousands of years. Within two days he declared that these locals would be useful to the Spanish as slaves or servants. Assuming he was in the East Indies, Columbus called them *indios,* Spanish for "Indians."

The locals spoke Arawak, so the Arabic and Hebrew translator he'd brought along was useless. Columbus communicated instead in crude sign language. He couldn't believe how kind and friendly the people were, even "loving" and "always laughing." He soon realized his advantage over them: "Weapons they have none, nor are acquainted with them, for I showed them swords which they grasped by the blades, and cut themselves through ignorance." He began handing out strings of beads and other small gifts, believing "that they could be much more easily converted to our holy faith by gentle means than by force."

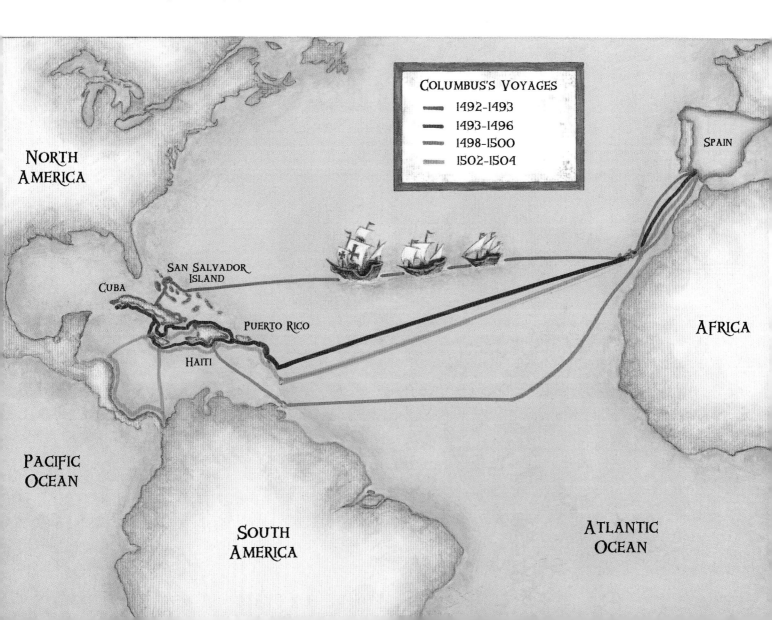

The local Indians helped Columbus in many ways, directing the ships to Cuba and then on to Haiti. Wherever he landed, he planted his flag, erected a cross made of trees, and promptly asked where the gold was. In his first two weeks on shore, his journal refers to gold sixteen times. Some Indians wore small nose rings of gold, and Columbus was positive large stores of it were just around the corner or over the horizon. Oddly, he hadn't brought any experts in metals along; the samples he gathered to take back were actually iron pyrite, also known as fool's gold.

Leaving a small settlement of Spaniards behind, Columbus sailed back to Spain. People were amazed that he'd returned at all. They marveled at his tales and at what he brought back: several Indians (most didn't survive the trip), parrots that talked and sang, spices, unfamiliar plants, fish of many colors, pineapples and other new fruits and vegetables.

Columbus swore he could find gold if he were allowed to return. Thanks to his new popularity, he sailed back with seventeen ships and some 1,300 men.

Columbus made four voyages in all, but with worsening results, mostly due to his cruelty when he became the appointed governor of the settlements. When he learned that Indians had killed some of his men, he began punishing the locals for small offenses by cutting off ears and noses. His hunt for gold intensified; he ordered that every male native over fourteen had to supply a specific amount of gold or get his hands cut off.

His acts of torture extended to his own crews, and so many men were inclined to rebel that he began hanging them for disobedience. Finally, Spain had Columbus arrested and brought home in chains. Amid charges of tyranny and incompetence, he was thrown in jail. He was released after six weeks and even received funding for another voyage, during which he was stranded and had to be rescued. His days as an explorer were over. Instead of working on maps or memoirs, he dressed as a monk in a scratchy brown robe and complained all the time.

He died two years later, probably at age fifty-four. He may have suffered from

Reiter's syndrome, with crippling arthritis, severe eye inflammation, and possibly some mental illness.

After his last voyage Columbus wrote, "Gold is most excellent. Gold is treasure, and whoever has it may do what he wishes in the world." His obsession made him oblivious to the other wonders he had seen—and he never knew that he had altered geography for all time.

ONWARD

⁓ Amerigo Vespucci, a merchant who supplied beef for Columbus's ships, later began leading his own explorations and lent his name to the whole continent: America.

⁓ Among the many things Columbus permanently changed about the world was food, in what has become known as the Columbian Exchange. From the Americas came maize, tobacco, potatoes, tomatoes, peanuts, pumpkins, chocolate, and much more, while Europeans in turn introduced their foods.

⁓ Reliable facts about Columbus are so few that many myths have sprung up. For example, it's probably not true that the crew on his first voyage threatened to throw him overboard. It's also not true that he reached what we consider the United States mainland; the closest he got was present-day Puerto Rico.

⁓ More places in America are named for Columbus than for anyone except George Washington. But he is not a hero to everyone. His actions began a process that almost wiped out the native population. Within one hundred years of Columbus's first encounter with the Indians, their numbers had been reduced by ninety percent.

FERDINAND MAGELLAN

BORN IN SABROSA, PORTUGAL, 1480(?)
DIED IN MACTAN, PHILIPPINES, 1521

Portuguese commander of the first expedition to circle the globe

The men and boys died in all kinds of ways. A few were executed; a few fell into the ocean from the ship's primitive toilet seat above the waves. At least twenty-nine died from the dreaded scurvy. Some starved to death, and some were killed when their unreliable weapons exploded in their faces. Many were ambushed by angry local inhabitants. Their leader, Ferdinand Magellan, ended up slashed into pieces.

A minor nobleman in Portugal, Magellan had been a page at court at age twelve. He was well-educated, from music and dance to math and navigation. Like his hero Columbus, he worked aboard ships, dreaming of making his own voyage and finding a way to the Spice Islands. He was convinced that there must be a sea route via an undiscovered passage or strait through South America. He petitioned his king over and over for funds, with no luck. By age thirty-seven, he was feeling middle-aged and impatient to sail, so he switched his loyalty from Portugal to its enemy Spain.

Spain was willing to gamble, allowing him a year to prepare an armada of five ships. Each was covered in tar, all black except for the sails. They held enough arms to equip a small army: cannons, hundreds of guns, three tons of gunpowder, hundreds of steel-tipped spikes. Magellan was short and had a permanent limp due to a severe knee injury. He made himself look more powerful with a deluxe suit of body armor, a helmet with bright feathers, six swords, and a red velvet chair he sat in for important meetings.

Magellan was all over the ships, even loading boxes like a common sailor. His crew and officers totaled more than 250 and hailed from Greece, Italy, France, North Africa, and Spain. They were mostly in their teens and twenties; Magellan was probably the oldest on board. He didn't speak Spanish well, and the Spaniards on board didn't like him. Neither did anyone else.

He brought his illegitimate son, Cristovao, with him, as well as a slave named Enrique. An Italian scholar, Antonio Pigafetta, was along; he kept a daily diary of the gruesome deaths. On board was a barber who also did all the dental and medical work, as well as a group of boys between eight and fifteen, mostly orphans, who chanted prayers in high voices as they turned the ships' hourglasses.

Magellan tried to show he was boss. As a warning, he ordered a sailor to strangle

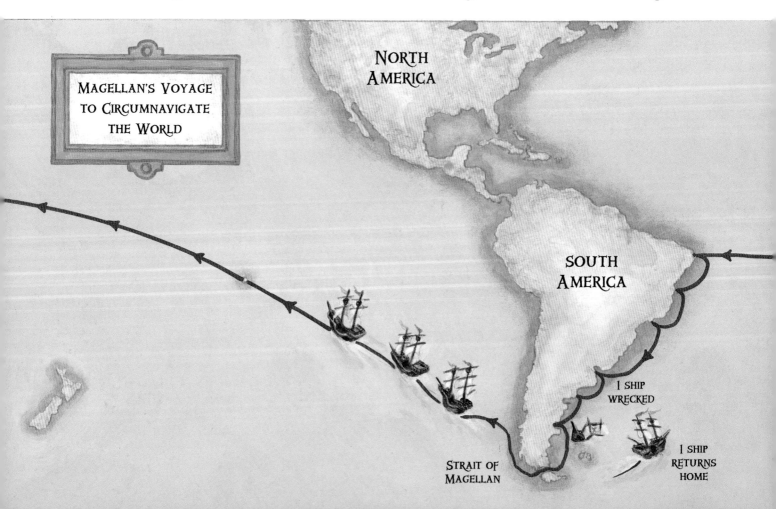

MAGELLAN'S VOYAGE
TO CIRCUMNAVIGATE
THE WORLD

NORTH
AMERICA

SOUTH
AMERICA

1 SHIP
WRECKED

STRAIT OF
MAGELLAN

1 SHIP
RETURNS
HOME

a rule-breaker in public—not a popular move. After six months he had lost the confidence of almost everyone. Mutineers took control of three of his ships, demanding to return home. Magellan managed to use his wits and weapons to put the rebellion down. He had the leader drawn and quartered, the body parts on display for months. Now he ruled by terror—using ghastly torture techniques borrowed from the Spanish Inquisition, ordering a servant to behead his master or die, marooning two men (one of them a priest) on a small island.

On they sailed across the Atlantic Ocean, on ships the crew nicknamed "flying pigs" because they were so filthy. Rats and mice were so numerous that sailors invented games to play with them. In the evenings the crew read books that had been approved by the Inquisition—lives of the saints or prayer books—or played practical jokes.

For months Magellan defied his rebellious men by trying again and again to find the strait he was sure existed. Finally, in 1520, he found it, between mainland

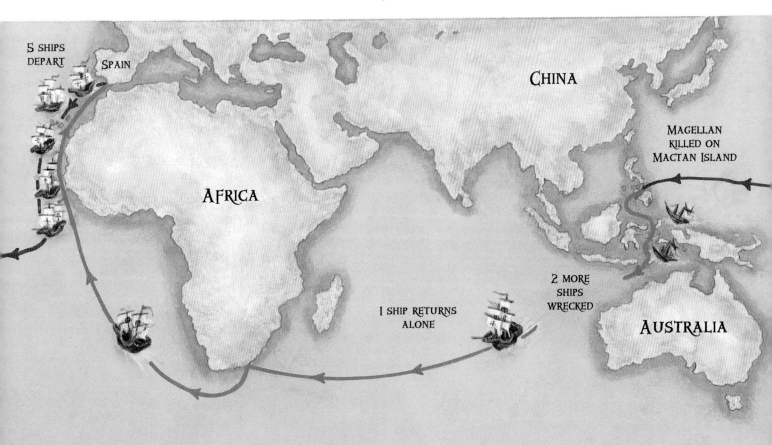

South America and Tierra del Fuego. A narrow strip of water leading mile after mile through sheer cliffs, it couldn't have been scarier. The sun was rarely visible. In some places, ancient walls of ice could fall onto the ships at any minute. Elsewhere, the men could sense eerie forests; did the fires they glimpsed mean that Indians were about to attack?

One of his vessels had been shipwrecked, but amazingly enough, Magellan was successful at steering the other four through the 325-mile passage.

After thirty-eight frightful days, they sailed out into open seas and found themselves in an entirely different ocean. Magellan called it Pacifico, or Pacific. "Everyone thought himself fortunate to be where none had been before," said one sailor. Magellan was so happy that he cried. Maybe now the Spice Islands were within reach.

But the mutiny was not over. The largest ship promptly broke away and sailed home without its leader. This was bad news—it had much of their food, and Magellan knew the mutineers would badmouth him back home for doing things like marooning a priest.

His three remaining ships sailed on for fourteen long weeks without encountering land. His men ate the last of the wormy biscuits, rat droppings mixed with wood shavings, and even the leather of their shoes. Scurvy attacked the crew but not the officers, whose quince jam was a source of vitamin C that protected them.

Magellan grew so frustrated that one day he hurled his maps overboard. After stopping in Guam, he still had no idea how to find the Spice Islands, resorting to asking directions from islanders rowing by.

When they reached the Philippines, Magellan became "blood brothers" with the king: each cut his chest, poured the mixed blood into a container of wine, and drank. Magellan's efforts to impress the locals by firing off artillery did not go over well; he scared them so much, they jumped off his boats into the ocean.

Then he started threatening death to those who refused baptism. Magellan was a devout Catholic, but conversion was not part of his official mission. Lapu Lapu, chief of the Philippine village of Mactan, refused—and Magellan attacked.

Fifteen hundred Mactanese warriors showed up, shooting poisoned arrows. Magellan ordered a retreat and kept fighting, but had already been shot in the leg. It's believed he kept looking back to make sure his men were getting to the boats, and then the warriors fell upon him. Neither his body nor armor was ever recovered.

In full-blown panic, the surviving crew fled—and continued to die in various ways. They were down to one ship when they made it back to Spain, having spent three years circling the entire globe. The ship was full of precious spices; they had eventually found their goal. But of the original crew, only about eighteen survived, many too weak upon arrival to talk or walk.

The discoveries of Ferdinand Magellan and his men had given Spain a major victory in world domination—but at an incredibly high cost.

ONWARD

⚬ Ten years after Magellan's death, the Strait of Magellan began to be named on maps. His navigation of it is considered one of the greatest accomplishments in the history of exploration.

⚬ Other attempts to travel around the world met with disaster, making Magellan's feat all the more startling. It took fifty-eight years for another explorer to do it: Francis Drake of England.

⚬ In the Philippines, Magellan is not considered a hero. Rather, an enormous statue of Lapu Lapu guards the Mactan harbor. Every April, thousands come to see the battle reenacted, with a movie star as Lapu Lapu and an ordinary soldier as Magellan.

⚬ Magellan's name has become a synonym for "explorer." An Internet search engine, a travel supply company, spacecraft, telescopes, a crater on Mars, and more have been named after him.

HENRY HUDSON

BORN IN ENGLAND, 1565(?)
DIED NEAR HUDSON BAY, NEW YORK, 1611(?)

English explorer of the New York area

Before he was about forty, almost nothing is known about Henry Hudson, perhaps the most stubborn explorer of all.

He was a professional sailor, probably with connections at England's court. He took his young son John to sea, leaving his wife, Katherine, and other sons behind in London. On his four voyages, he was obsessed with finding passage to Asia. Other explorers shared his goal, but Hudson tried more routes than anyone else. Still, aboard his most famous ship, the *Half Moon,* lived a cat, and the night it went screaming across the deck proved to be a bad omen for him.

Some of his financial backers were irritated with his "strange behavior"; he didn't always follow instructions. Both deceitful and charming, he played people off each other. But the English and Dutch kept funding his trips because he didn't ask for much money in advance, never lost a ship, rarely lost a man, and never got trapped by ice and had to "overwinter" (wait until spring arrived to continue). And he was an outstanding navigator.

Along the coast of what became New York, starting possibly on Long Island, Hudson began charting areas later named for him. He was impressed by the plentiful fish, wildflowers, forests, and possible sources of copper. The local Indian tribes met the ships with dancing and singing and trading. "It is as pleasant a land as one need tread upon," Hudson said.

On his final voyage, aboard the Dutch-funded *Discovery*, Hudson sailed back and forth in James Bay, looking for that passage to Asia, confident that success was at hand and China was nearby.

In his crew, the Dutch outnumbered their rivals, the English, by three to one. Hudson became so paranoid that the Dutch would steal his ship that he hardly ever left it. Now, for the first time, his ship and crew were forced to overwinter, surrounded by ice, and the tension grew. Hudson became isolated and secretive; he was even accused of hoarding food for himself.

When the ice finally broke, the crew ambushed Hudson. They forced him, his son John, and any sick sailors into a small open boat with some supplies. Then they cut the rope, setting them adrift. For a while Hudson and the others rowed frantically after the ship, but they were left behind. Hudson, at about age forty-four, was soon presumed dead.

The Dutch didn't make a fuss about what happened to Hudson. He hadn't reached Asia and he hadn't returned. But Holland now established claim to what it named New Amsterdam, later known as New York, which became the largest port city on the east coast and the entry to America.

James Cook

Born in Marton, Yorkshire, England, 1728
Died in Kealakekua Bay, Hawaii, 1779

English explorer who mapped much of the Southern Hemisphere

James Cook once wrote that he intended to go not only "farther than any man has been before me, but as far as I think it is possible for a man to go." It was all about the "pleasure of being first."

Such an ambitious man advanced quickly in the Royal Navy, which was so important to Britain that it took up sixty percent of the national budget. Having gone to sea as a teen, Cook had studied all forms of math, navigation, and astronomy—though he never learned to swim. His talent for charting, honed under often terrible conditions, brought him to the attention of those in power at a key moment in the history of British discovery. He was the right man at the right time.

At age thirty-nine, he was made commander of a voyage to Tahiti, New Zealand (a twelve-year-old sailor was the first to sight it), Australia, and more, charting and taking possession as he sailed.

Captain Cook was picky about his crew. He wanted men who were easy to get along with as well as skilled. He rejected one cook as being too frail, and wasn't happy with another the navy told him to hire, a man with one hand.

By all accounts Cook was an inspirational, respected leader. One sailor called him "most friendly, benevolent, and humane." Another thought of him as "a kind of superior being." He had a stern side and sometimes seemed in a world of his own; he could eat dinner with his officers without saying a word. But many men were happy to sail with him on all three of his trips.

He maintained discipline by whipping a rule-breaker strapped to a barrel. One day he gave a man twelve lashes for refusing to eat fresh beef, which Cook insisted was healthier than the salted meat the sailor preferred. This proved such a powerful example that there were only twenty-one more whippings on all three voyages. Trying to desert was the worst offense: twenty-four lashes.

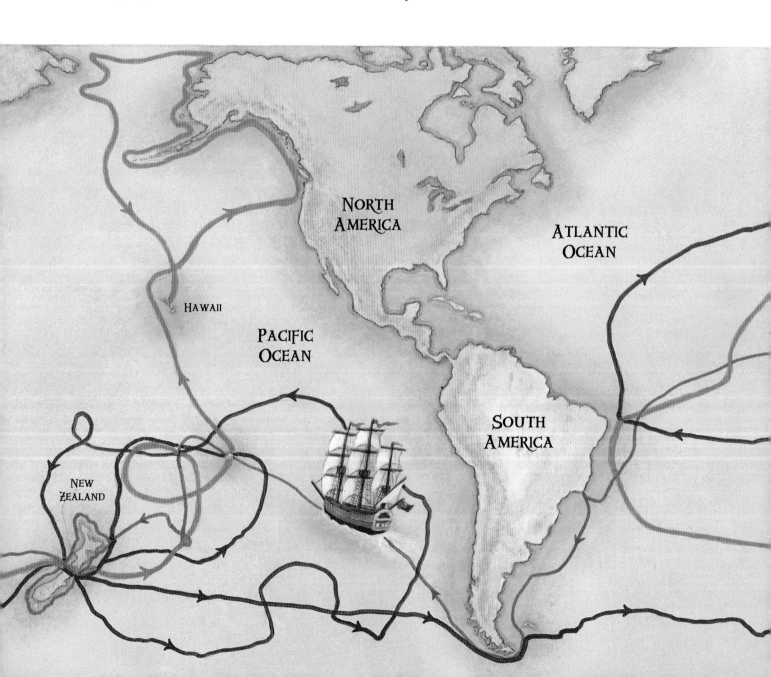

Even with plenty of alcohol on board—enormous amounts of rum, literally tons of beer—there was little violence on Cook's ships. He never drank or partied like the others. He had been brought up as a Quaker, but he never mentioned religion, seldom went to church, never allowed clergy on board, and performed his religious tasks on ship in a dutiful fashion.

His concern for the health of his crew was so great that he was able to stay at sea longer than explorers before him. He installed a platform where officers could exercise and was fierce about cleanliness. Sailors grumbled about washing clothes often and

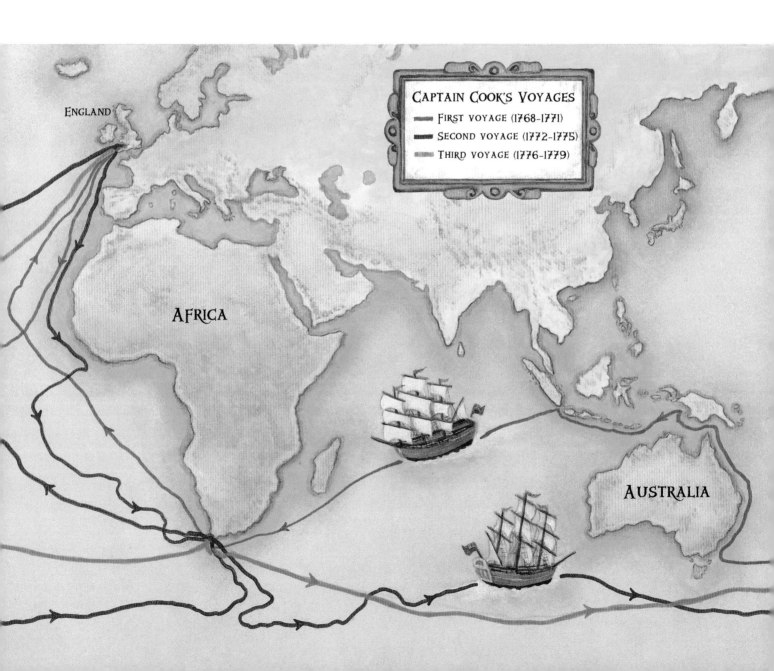

having to swab decks all the time. Those who kept monkeys were dismayed when Cook ordered the pets tossed overboard because he didn't like their droppings.

Cook's courage was obvious: he would walk unarmed into crowds of hostile local inhabitants to show he meant no harm. He was gentler with locals than other explorers were, always striving to do the right thing.

At first he was unfazed by cannibals he encountered. He saw their practice as an ancient custom they wouldn't be able to break: "If they have more of their enemies than they can eat, they throw them into the sea." He was less accepting after the discovery of the remains of eleven of his crew, who had been captured and eaten while out collecting wild greens.

Whenever Cook returned home, honors and titles were heaped upon him. He was greatly expanding Europe's knowledge of the globe using the first-ever chronometer, which allowed him to measure longitude. He published his travel journals and gained more fame. When not at sea, Cook lived in a modest house with a garden, next to a gin distillery. He was always a dutiful son, faithful to his wife, Elizabeth, and attentive to their six children, though they were never together more than a couple of months at a time.

On his third voyage, Cook explored Hawaii. He was the first European to land there. His behavior seemed to change, perhaps from exhaustion. He could not stop vomiting, apparently suffering from parasites or a similar stomach ailment.

He seemed irrational to his crew. One day he ordered the slaughter of a flock of walruses in order to have fresh meat—a bloody affair that disgusted many. The men found the cooked walrus meat totally inedible, but anyone who refused to eat it was allowed nothing else but biscuits.

As arguments broke out between the Europeans and Hawaiians, Cook began punishing any locals who stole from them by cutting off their ears. His crew was shocked. When two of his goats were stolen, Cook went on an uncharacteristic rampage, setting twenty houses and many boats on fire.

The theft of one of his small boats seemed to be the last straw. In a move that was possibly suicidal, Cook deliberately challenged the islanders in an attempt to take the king of Hawaii hostage. During the fight, he was unable to get from the beach to his boat; he still hadn't learned how to swim. As Cook turned his back on the Hawaiians to signal the boat to come to him, villagers struck him on the head and stabbed him to death.

His men were unable to believe that their legendary leader was dead at age fifty. They sailed home to England as fast as possible.

Elizabeth lived on for another fifty-six years, financially comfortable owing to Cook's pension and the profits from his books.

ONWARD

Cook was the first explorer to squash scurvy; he lost not a single crew member to the disease. The carrot marmalade he packed was popular with the crew, but the thousands of pounds of pickled cabbage, or sauerkraut, was not. His men loathed it, but Cook made eating it mandatory. Not until 1932 was scurvy proven to be caused by a deficiency in vitamin C, supplied by certain fruits and vegetables.

Cook always brought along scientists and artists. Thanks to a botanist on board, Cook increased the world's knowledge of thousands of plants never before recorded.

The eastern coast of Australia was one of the last places unmapped by Europeans. While exploring, Cook named dozens of its bays and other features. Eighteen years later, Britain sent convicts from its jails to establish its first colony there.

DANIEL BOONE

BORN IN BERKS COUNTY, PENNSYLVANIA, 1734
DIED IN SAINT CHARLES, MISSOURI, 1820

American outdoorsman who opened the way west to Kentucky and onward

Daniel Boone was sometimes caught singing to himself in the forest. That's how happy being in uncharted woods made him.

After he received his first rifle at age twelve, he vanished into the hills along the North Carolina frontier. Mastering the hunting skills he learned from local Europeans and American Indians, he kept his family stuffed with venison, rabbits, squirrels, turkey. (His own favorite meal was the liver of an elk, garnished with sweet potatoes.) He could read tracks, droppings, and bent twigs, and became expert at fading into the forest to evade hostile Indians. He earned money by selling furs and hunting for ginseng root, an herbal medicine that he could sell to the local Chinese for a big profit.

At sixteen he took his first long trip, exploring hundreds of miles of wilderness with a friend. Reportedly, he killed ninety-one bears during one winter, and he and a friend killed thirty deer in one day. Boone most often preferred to travel alone with a horse and a dog.

By his late teens, Boone was legendary. Like Paul Bunyan, he became the subject of so many tall tales that some now doubt he was a real person. As he put it, "Many heroic actions and chivalrous adventures are related of me which exist only in

the regions of fancy. With me the world has taken great liberties, and yet I have been but a common man."

As a wandering hunter and trapper, Boone became interested in mapping geography. He had an incredible memory and never forgot a place he'd been. It's believed he didn't use a compass; he navigated by using the sun and stars and other clues in nature. He probably knew every inch of his surrounding territory better than any other white man. "I can't say as ever I was lost," he joked, "but I was bewildered once for three days."

No wonder Boone was hired to help blaze a trail through Cumberland Gap, hundreds of miles long, as yet uncharted. What lay beyond? No one knew exactly, but it was rumored to be glorious. The plan was to establish the area as Kentucky, a new state. With fertile land and abundant game, Kentucky sounded like paradise to Boone. His dream was to live there peacefully with the Indian inhabitants.

He set to work hacking a path wide enough for horses. This would become the Wilderness Road, the main route to the West. Boone helped establish Boonesborough, the first settlement in Kentucky, and soon brought his wife, Rebecca, and their family to join him there.

Boone had met Rebecca when he was nineteen and she was fifteen. Tough and feisty, she was a capable hunter herself. He considered her his rock, though his travels took him away from her for long periods of time. Once, after he'd been gone for two years, she presented him with a new daughter, Jemima, who though not his own became his favorite of his many children. He was an affectionate father and sometimes took his oldest son, James, hunting, "hugging up to him" on winter nights to keep him warm. Raised as a Quaker, Boone did not attend church but considered himself a Christian.

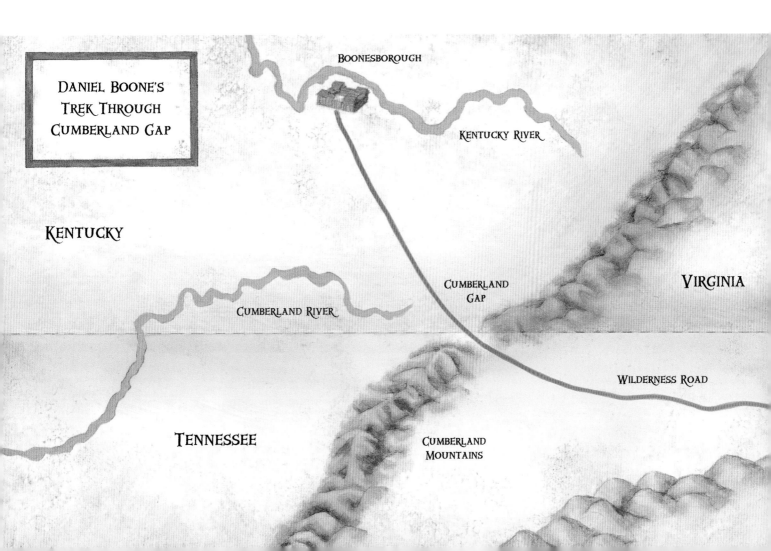

DANIEL BOONE'S
TREK THROUGH
CUMBERLAND GAP

BOONESBOROUGH

KENTUCKY RIVER

KENTUCKY

CUMBERLAND RIVER

CUMBERLAND
GAP

VIRGINIA

WILDERNESS ROAD

TENNESSEE

CUMBERLAND
MOUNTAINS

Boone's education was sketchy (spelling was always a bugbear), but he took books with him on trips. His favorites were the Bible, *Gulliver's Travels,* and history books. He was often the only literate person in a group of explorers and would read aloud to them around the campfire at night.

Someone described him as "a remarkably pleasant good-natured mannerly man." Everyone liked him; he was witty, told jokes and stories, and avoided talk of politics. Cherokee Indians named him Wide Mouth because of his laughter. He almost always had his guard up and in emergencies stayed cool.

His relationship with the various tribes he encountered was mixed. His parents had been friendly to Indians and often fed and sheltered those passing through. Boone respected Indians and was respected by them. He maintained this stance even after he was shot in the knee in an Indian attack, his son James was tortured and killed by Indians, and his daughter Jemima was kidnapped by an Indian war party. (Boone rescued her two days later.)

He himself was captured and held by Shawnee Indians for four months. The chief, Blackfish, adopted Boone as a son and gave him the name Big Turtle. When Boone learned that Blackfish was about to attack Boonesborough with a large force, he escaped to warn the settlement. Traveling the 160 miles on horseback—and, after his horse gave out, on foot—took five days. He made bandages of oak bark for his bleeding feet and built a hasty raft to cross a river. He reached the town in time and helped defend it during a ten-day siege.

As resourceful as he was, Boone had trouble prospering. He earned money by locating good land for other settlers, running a tavern, trading horses, and selling furs. But he was terrible with money, and his sense of honor made him reluctant to profit at someone else's expense. He was also unlucky. At one point he was master of thirty thousand acres and ended up losing it all. He owned slaves whenever he could afford them, and at one time had seven. He didn't pay his taxes, was sued many times, and once had a warrant out for his arrest. Though he was always deep in debt, he was determined to pay off all his debts eventually—and did so.

Daniel Boone died of natural causes at age eighty-five, surrounded by children, grandchildren, and neighbors, who all adored him. Until the end he remained keenly interested in explorations west, dreaming about the Pacific Coast.

ONWARD

Cumberland Gap allowed hundreds of thousands of people to follow Boone and open up the West. His lifetime spanned an explosion in the American population, from fewer than one million to ten million. He was aware that he had caused much of the westward expansion, and feared that this was wrecking the wilderness he loved.

Boone's name has long represented the American outdoors. A group called Sons of Daniel Boone was the earliest version of the Boy Scouts of America.

The *Daniel Boone* series on TV in the late 1960s is the source of some of the myths about him. On TV, Boone was called a "big man" in a coonskin cap and the "rippin'est, roarin'est, fightin'est man the frontier ever knew!" In real life, Boone was short, hated coonskin caps (he always wore a hat made of beaver felt), and rarely lost his temper.

MERIWETHER LEWIS, WILLIAM CLARK, AND SACAJAWEA

BORN NEAR CHARLOTTESVILLE, VIRGINIA, 1774; DIED NEAR NASHVILLE, TENNESSEE, 1809 (LEWIS)
BORN IN CAROLINE COUNTY, VIRGINIA, 1770; DIED IN SAINT LOUIS, MISSOURI, 1838 (CLARK)
BORN IN IDAHO OR MONTANA, 1788(?); DIED IN FORT MANUEL, NORTH DAKOTA, 1812 (SACAJAWEA)

Two American explorers and their Shoshone Indian interpreter on an epic journey

Meriwether Lewis and William Clark had much in common. Both were well-to-do Virginia planters, slaveholders, and army veterans. They were four years apart in age and got along well. So when President Thomas Jefferson asked Captain Lewis to explore the giant parcel of land known as the Louisiana Purchase, Lewis chose Clark to be his co-captain. They were to set out from St. Louis, Missouri, leaving the known United States behind, heading west with the nearly impossible goal of crossing the Rocky Mountains and reaching the Pacific Ocean.

Sacajawea had virtually nothing in common with either Lewis or Clark. But they could not have made their journey without her.

Lewis had grown up fast, taking care of his family and managing his plantation at a young age. He was a skilled hunter and well-educated, keenly interested in natural history and medicinal herbs. At least one of his neighbors admired him—President Jefferson, who praised his "luminous and discriminating intellect" and hired him as his secretary. Lewis mixed with big names in politics and the arts, polished his manners, and learned to dance.

But, despite actively trying, he never married. "His person was stiff and without grace," said a cousin, "bow-legged, awkward, formal, and almost without flexibility."

Another man called him "an overgrown baby." Some historians think Lewis suffered bouts of depression. Even James Madison's bubbly wife, Dolley, couldn't match him up. Lewis started referring to himself as "a musty, fusty, rusty, old bachelor."

Redheaded Clark was more amiable and less moody than Lewis. He had little formal education—he spelled "Sioux" twenty-seven different ways—but was a big reader of geography and history as well as novels. After his journey with Lewis, he married twice, had eight children, and was a founding member of his local Episcopal church. But he treated slaves cruelly, and bragged that they remained with him even after they'd been offered freedom.

To prepare for their journey west, Lewis and Clark added thirty-eight members to their group, called the Corps of Discovery. The men had to be "stout" (healthier than the average American), good hunters or able to offer another necessary skill, unmarried, and able to withstand harsh conditions over two years. The youngest was seventeen; the oldest, thirty-five. All were white except Clark's slave, York. Lewis's Newfoundland dog, Seaman, went along. Their provisions included a vast assortment of gifts for the Indians they would encounter, 120 gallons of alcohol, and a great deal of medicine. (With 600 mercury capsules used as laxatives, it is said the Corps's path can still be traced by way of mercury deposits in the soil.)

The day of departure in 1804 was among the happiest of Lewis's life. In his journal he dared to compare himself to Columbus and Cook, and said, "We were now about to penetrate a country at least two thousand miles in width, on which the foot of civilized man had never trodden; the good or evil it had in store for us was for experiment yet to determine."

The Corps would face threats both expected (grizzly bears) and unpredictable (blinding blizzards). They carried the latest in weaponry, though they were under strict orders from Jefferson to avoid fighting. To keep order, the leaders imposed military discipline, with punishments (a hundred lashes for breaking into the liquor supply, for example) and rewards (extra whiskey rations or getting out of guard duty).

On good days the men ate well, dining on fish, buffalo, elk, or deer, along with roots and berries. Sometimes they were reduced to eating wild dog, which Clark hated; some days there was no food at all and they ate their candles.

Along the way, the men met a French-Canadian fur trader and his Shoshone Indian wife—Sacajawea, or Bird Woman. Taken captive by a rival tribe when she was younger, she was now fifteen years old, pregnant, and articulate in several languages. Joining the expedition along with her husband, she became valuable as an interpreter, helping to negotiate with the Shoshone and the dozens of other Indian nations they encountered.

What did Indians think of the Corps? The white men, who rarely bathed, struck them as smelly. Were they too poor to dress in blankets, as the Indians did? And were they eating themselves when they reached into their pockets (unknown to Indians) for snacks of jerky or bits of cold food left over from last night's dinner? Were their intentions good or evil?

Trying to show that they meant well, one Corps member brought along his fiddle, which sometimes got Americans and Indians dancing together around the campfire at night.

But the key to peace was usually Sacajawea. Besides translating, Sacajawea was indispensable just for her presence. The sight of a woman and her newborn baby went a long way toward easing tensions, showing that the expedition was not there to fight. The Corps needed Indian help, and thanks in large part to Sacajawea, they got it.

She came to their rescue often, digging up nourishing roots, several times saving them from starving to death. When they were in areas she knew from her childhood, she guided them. Once she grabbed things from an overturned boat, including the journals of Lewis and Clark. Another day she gave up her blue beaded belt so the leaders could trade it for a fur robe to bring back to Jefferson.

Sacajawea helped them with their biggest challenge—crossing the Rocky Mountains, which were much trickier than they'd anticipated. The group was baffled

ROCKY
MOUNTAINS

YELLOWSTONE RIVER

PACIFIC
OCEAN

COLUMBIA RIVER

LEWIS AND CLARK EXPEDITION
DEPARTED ST. LOUIS MAY 1804
REACHED THE PACIFIC OCEAN NOVEMBER 1805
RETURNED TO ST. LOUIS SEPTEMBER 1806

and in danger of getting lost until the day they encountered a band of Shoshones. Sacajawea started dancing and laughing. The chief was none other than her own brother, whom she hadn't seen since childhood. Thanks to the happy reunion of the siblings, Lewis and Clark had no trouble negotiating for the horses and guides they needed to make the passage through the Rockies.

Clark fondly called Sacajawea's baby his "little dancing boy, Pomp," while Lewis referred to the baby as "it" in his journal. Perhaps that's why Sacajawea was friendlier with Clark; she would do him favors and go for walks with him, often showing him which plants to collect. If he caught Sacajawea's husband hitting her, Clark would yell at him.

She and the men were often sick, but in preparation for the trip, the two leaders

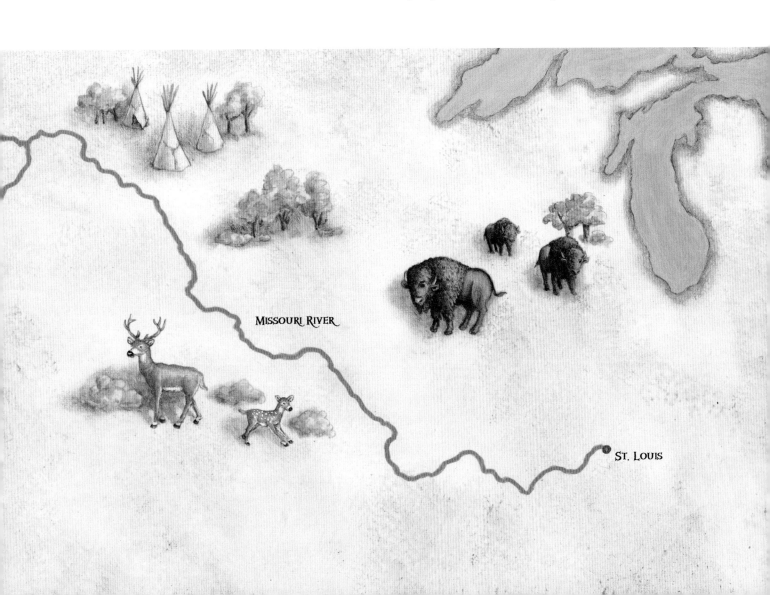

MISSOURI RIVER

ST. LOUIS

had studied medicine with the most well-known doctors in America. Lewis and Clark knew as much as most civilian doctors of the day and could treat common ailments, reset bones, remove bullets, do blood-letting, and give shots. Once one of his own men mistook Lewis for an elk and fired, injuring him in the thigh and backside. Many people back home gave up the Corps for dead, yet only one man actually died, from infection after a ruptured appendix. Luck was almost always on their side—the trip could have gone far differently.

The most serious confrontation the Corps met was on the day a band of Sioux tried to block their way. After gifts, the Indians were finally persuaded to move aside.

After a year, the Corps did reach the Pacific Ocean. Sacajawea gave her opinion about where they should spend the winter and insisted on visiting the ocean to see a beached whale. After exploring the West Coast of America, the group returned to Saint Louis.

It was 1806, and the Corps had traveled 8,000 miles. They brought back a huge amount of new information, about 140 precious maps, and more than 200 plants and animals new to science. And they helped establish the idea that the United States was destined to expand all the way to the Pacific.

Lewis and Clark promptly went shopping for new clothes and underwear. They were each rewarded with a promotion and 1,600 acres of land. Some members of the Corps stayed in the military, while others entered the fur trade or returned to farming.

Lewis, while trying to get his journals published, had trouble adjusting to life as an ex-explorer. Suffering from bad bouts of malaria, he may have been poisoned by the large doses of mercury he took to treat it. Or perhaps his depression overwhelmed him; there are hints in his journals that he felt like a failure. He died at age thirty-five, most likely a suicide, while traveling to meet with a publisher.

Most historians believe that Sacajawea died of a fever at about age twenty-five, three years after Lewis. She had given birth to a daughter who probably died in childhood. Clark became the guardian of her son and provided him with the best education possible.

The only one of the three to have a full life after their adventure, Clark continued to work for the government. He turned part of his house into a tourist attraction full of Indian artifacts. When he died at sixty-eight, he was Superintendent of Indian Affairs, overseeing the transfer of millions of acres from Indians to white Americans.

ONWARD

If you live in the states of Washington, Idaho, Oregon, Missouri, Kansas, North or South Dakota, Nebraska, Iowa, or Montana—you have Lewis and Clark to thank. Their journey was the key to the westward expansion of America. On the other hand, their trip was the beginning of the end of Indian ownership of this land.

Today we tend to refer to them as one word—"LewisandClark"—and no American explorers are more famous. But the expedition was largely ignored until the publicity of the 1904 Louisiana Purchase Exposition in Saint Louis. The bicentennial of the journey in the year 2000 elevated their fame.

In 2001, Sacajawea was posthumously made an Honorary Sergeant, Regular Army, by President Bill Clinton. Clinton also promoted Clark to the rank of Captain (Lewis had been a captain and had called Clark captain out of respect).

Lewis's cause of death is still disputed. The debate about whether to exhume his body for testing went back and forth for years, but a 2010 ruling by the Department of the Interior was final: He and the pioneers buried near him cannot be disturbed.

RICHARD FRANCIS BURTON

BORN IN TORQUAY, DEVONSHIRE, ENGLAND, 1821
DIED IN TRIESTE, ITALY, 1890

English explorer of the Middle East and Africa

Forever controversial, Richard Burton inspired whispers among his neighbors. Some found him demonic; others thought he was merely scary. Said one man, "He reminded me of a black leopard, caged but unforgiving . . . a countenance the most sinister I have ever seen, dark, cruel, treacherous, with eyes like a wild beast's."

But Sir Burton was actually a distinguished English scholar and explorer. "Discovery is mostly my mania," he said. He prided himself on knowing things most people didn't, especially about religions (he was obsessed with Islam) and the paranormal (he was the first to use the term ESP). As a young man he learned twenty-five languages, mastering dialects that eventually expanded the number to forty.

After he was expelled from Oxford University for a minor offense (having deliberately tried to get kicked out), he joined the English forces in Pakistan as an officer, working as a spy. Dressed as a Muslim merchant, he would haunt the bazaars, writing his observations on tiny squares of paper.

Burton was the first European to explore parts of Africa and the Middle East that had been closed to outsiders. He took an enormous bright yellow umbrella into the desert for sun protection. Disguised as an Afghanistani Muslim, he was often in great danger and could have been executed if he'd been caught. But he never was, even when he journeyed into the sacred city of Mecca, where he took notes and made sketches of the holy Muslim shrine.

Burton was crossing Somalia in search of the source of the Nile River when his camp was attacked. A javelin struck him, the point piercing one cheek and exiting the other. Burton's priority was escape. The weapon stayed in his face until it could be removed the next day, leaving him with a serious scar and several missing teeth. On another trip, Burton trekked across Africa, suffering one calamity after another. When he finally arrived at Lake Tanganyika (which he believed, wrongly, was the source of the Nile), he was so ill from malaria that he couldn't walk, though he later recovered.

At age forty he married Isabel Arundell in a secret ceremony; her aristocratic Catholic family disapproved. She didn't mind when he practiced hypnotism on her.

Despite his hair-raising adventures, Burton never actually killed anyone and got irritated when people assumed he had. A doctor once asked, "How do you feel when you have killed a man?" Burton answered sarcastically, "Quite jolly. What about you?"

He once complained, "England is the only country where I never feel at home." He spent his final years in Italy, sharing his discoveries by writing dozens of books. He had a separate desk for each project, the most famous being a translation of *The Thousand and One Nights* or *The Arabian Nights*, which introduced this classic to the West.

Skeletal and scarred after his hard life, Burton died of a heart attack at age sixty-nine. Isabel, well aware of her husband's racy reputation, burned almost all forty years' worth of his journals.

Gun or No Gun?

Isabella Bird

Born in North Yorkshire, England, 1831
Died in Edinburgh, Scotland, 1904

English explorer who traveled more than any other woman before her time

The Royal Geographical Society was just so stuffy. "We contest the general capability of women to contribute to scientific geographical knowledge," sneered one of its men. He called women "unfitted for exploration," and declared that the fact that some were doing it anyway was "one of the horrors of the latter end of the nineteenth century."

Women were not supposed to do whatever they liked, much less travel—and traveling alone was all but unheard of. Isabella Bird felt guilty about it, fearing that she should spend her time helping others instead. The daughter of a Church of England minister and a Sunday school teacher, she was devoutly religious.

But when she stayed home she was always in pain. Doctors disagreed about a solution. Should she wear a steel net to help support her head and spare her spine? Should she avoid walking up or down stairs? Would the motion of a boat help with the pain?

Following this particular lead, her father let twenty-two-year-old Isabella sail from England to visit relatives in America. He gave her money and said she could stay as long her funds lasted.

Isabella felt better, so after her visit to America she just kept on moving. She preferred to travel to places as yet unmapped—no cities, nothing touristy: "I am doing what a woman can hardly ever do—leading a life fit to recruit a man. . . . I feel energy for anything except conventionality and civilization." At first, to seem proper, Bird used her health as her excuse for travel. Her ailments had a way of improving whenever she took off: "No door bells, no 'please ma'ams,' no dirt, no servants, no bills, no demands of any kind. . . . Above all, no nervousness and no conventionalities."

But eventually Bird wanted to be taken seriously as an explorer. She sought new worlds "so pure, so fresh, so vital, so careless, so unfettered, so full of interest that one grudges being asleep."

Bird's early explorations included Australia (she disliked it), Hawaii (she adored it), and Colorado, the newest American state and mostly unexplored. There her braids froze to her head after she washed her hair outdoors in the freezing weather. More enjoyable was meeting Rocky Mountain Jim, a magnetic outlaw with one eye (the other had been taken out by a grizzly bear). On the dangerous climb to Pike's

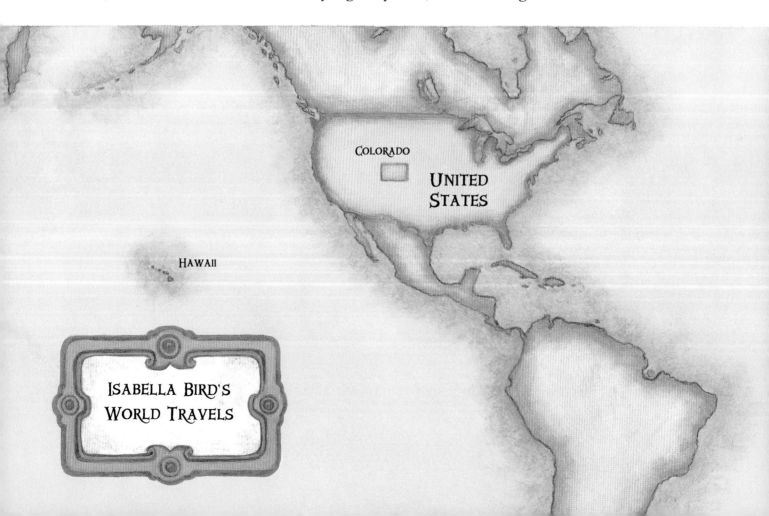

COLORADO

UNITED
STATES

HAWAII

ISABELLA BIRD'S
WORLD TRAVELS

Peak, he hoisted Bird onto his shoulders so she could see the view. In snowy valleys he romped with her and his collie hunting dog, Ring.

She fell in love, but Rocky Mountain Jim really was wild: "He is a man whom any woman might love but no sane woman would marry." She wrote him a formal letter to break off their relationship ("It is my wish that our acquaintance shall at once terminate") and he was killed in a fight the following year.

Picky about companions, Bird usually traveled alone: "Solitude is infinitely preferable to uncongeniality, and is bliss when compared with repulsiveness." She wrote letters home to Henrietta, her sister and best friend. They had private jokes and a secret language—"annoying" was code for when a man was too persistent; "dil" was a dull person—and Henrietta gave Isabella all the stability she needed.

The more primitive the surroundings, the more exhilarated Bird was. Besides her taste for danger, she had a gift for writing. She turned her letters to her sister into books that were witty, precise, and thoroughly researched. She named every plant

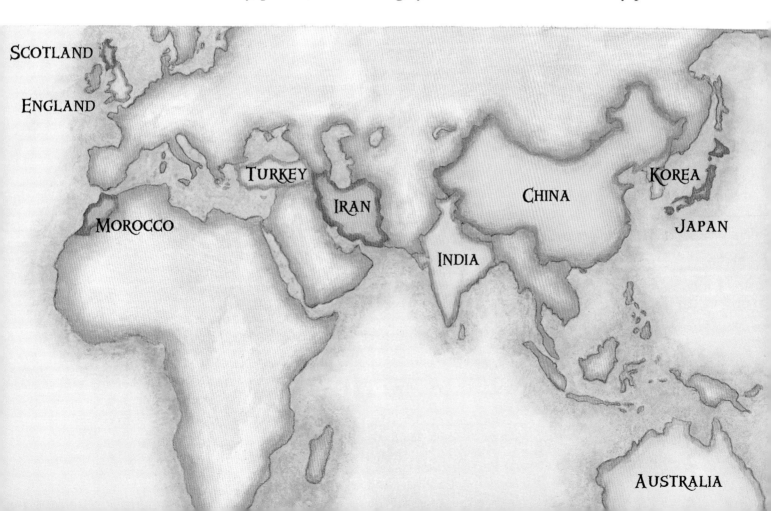

she saw, included geographic and historical details, provided maps. She used all five senses to make a scene come alive in "you are there" fashion. After groaning one day about the rattlesnakes around her cabin (one of which she had just killed), she wrote, "And besides snakes, the earth and air are alive and noisy with forms of insect life, large and small, stinging, humming, buzzing, striking, rasping, devouring!"

Her books—ten in all, later illustrated with her excellent photos—became bestsellers as well as standard reference books. Reviewers praised them as an experience akin to being in an exotic location; readers could skip the difficulties of the actual journey.

Bird was under five feet tall, not glamorous, and never lost her dignity or respectability even when she was shot at, encountered bears, endured earthquakes, or was flipped off her horse or camel. She went to places no European woman had gone or where all foreigners were hated; there she often coped with people taunting her, spitting or throwing stones, trying to break down her door, or spying on her through chinks in her walls. A minister who knew her said, "Her absolute unconsciousness of fear was a remarkable characteristic."

Bird disdained carrying a gun at first, but in time saw that it often saved her life. All she had to do was pull it out and pretend to check the bullets, or let it be known that she kept it under her pillow. Other indispensable travel items were cocoa, tea, raisins, a lamp for reading, her Bible, and a black silk dress for special occasions. She got angry when she was accused of wearing men's clothes, which she never did. But she did realize, on her way to a volcano she was frantic to see, how silly it was to ride sidesaddle instead of astride, like a man. Riding astride was much more comfortable.

On one of her most dangerous trips, she worked with an English army officer to map what was later Turkey and Iran. These large areas of the map had previously been marked "Unknown" and "Empty." After galloping three hundred miles across land with no roads, she wrote, "With my cranky spine I have become a greater horsewoman than ever!" The trip was so tough that she lost thirty-two pounds, but she bounced back and later addressed the British Parliament about her discoveries.

Bird was heartbroken when Henrietta died, but then married Henrietta's doctor. At forty, John Bishop was ten years younger and called her explorations "outlandish," but promised never to stop her. They went weeks without seeing each other due to her travels; he died after five years of devotion to her.

Bird promptly embarked on some of her most harrowing trips: Korea, China, Japan, India. She studied medicine so she could work at mission hospitals, wrote more amazing books, and was useful wherever she went. "I think I have contributed so much to the sum of general knowledge of different countries," she declared, "that had I been a man, I should undoubtably have received some recognition from the Royal Geographical Society."

When the Society eventually wanted her to give a speech, she refused; some of the members (still all men) had far fewer credentials than she did. Finally they named her their first woman "fellow" and admitted fifteen other women. Bird became the first woman to address the Society, as spellbinding a speaker as she was a writer.

At age sixty-nine she took off for Morocco, but heart disease was beginning to weaken her. Isabella Bird died three years later, her trunk packed for another trip to China.

ONWARD

Bird's *Adventures in the Rocky Mountains*—a modern classic read in women's studies, geology, geography, anthropology, and history classes—has inspired others to follow in her footsteps in Colorado.

A line of clothing especially for female travelers is named for her: Territory Ahead's Isabella Bird apparel.

The Royal Geographical Society's decision to allow women to join was so controversial that the following year they reversed it. Women were barred again for a while, except for those original sixteen. Today the Society still supports exploration and has 15,000 members, including many women.

BODY PARTS ON THE CEILING

MARY KINGSLEY

BORN IN LONDON, ENGLAND, 1862
DIED NEAR CAPE TOWN, SOUTH AFRICA, 1900

English explorer of little-known parts of Africa

Young Mary Kingsley was mostly on her own; she even had to teach herself to read. Fortunately, she had access to her father's impressive library. She loved memoirs, with lots of maps, by explorers Burton, Cook, and Bird. She lacked the confidence to go anywhere herself: "It never occurs to me that I have any right to do anything more than, now and then, sit and warm myself at the fire of real human beings."

Her father, a doctor, was almost always away, and her mother was an invalid who never left her room. At age five, Mary was already taking care of the housework. Her life in her quiet English village consisted of ministering to her mother's every need. Between chores, she fantasized about the African tropics.

When Kingsley was about thirty, both parents died the same year and she, rather recklessly, decided to escape. She later said she was "dead tired and feeling no one had need of me anymore. . . . I went down to West Africa to die." It was an unthinkable journey, with doctors warning that the local diseases made her destination "the deadliest spot on earth."

Still on the ship, she wrote a friend, "I have been having a wild time," just after she found her cabin loaded up with four male corpses that the crew couldn't fit anywhere else. Once in Africa, she was shown two newly dug graves and told they were always kept ready for Europeans.

It was too late to scare her off. Kingsley was already in love with the gigantic butterflies and dragonflies; the people; the whole colorful continent. She went on to explore many parts of Africa, including places never seen by any European. She transformed herself from a shy recluse into someone who could wade for hours through swamps, up to her neck in black slime. She would emerge covered in leeches, weak from loss of blood—and still able to laugh at herself.

Her way of exploring was to pose as a trader, carrying glass beads, fishhooks, toothbrushes. She used small items to befriend those who had never seen a white woman with light-blond hair; trading helped her get to know them and learn more. She traveled lightly, without fanfare, always by walking or paddling a canoe, not carried by servants like other Europeans.

Kingsley often went into hazardous, uncharted areas alone, learning as much as she could about tribes untouched by European influence—even tribes with a repu-

tation for cannibalism. When a stench kept her awake one night, she searched her dwelling and found small bags hanging from the ceiling. Inside were a freshly cut human hand, eyeballs, ears, and toes. Assuming that they were part of a local tradition, she merely put the bags carefully back where she had found them.

Another time, Kingsley saw "four human heads apparently floating on the mud," but then realized they were just fishermen coming out of the water to greet her. She was almost always treated well. Once she came upon seven African men who seemed to be having a ceremony. She took off, fearing they'd kill her for witnessing a secret ritual, but they caught her and explained they were only monkey-hunting.

The Africans' most frequent question was to ask why she was traveling without a man. Kingsley learned to point ahead, as though indicating that she was catching up to her (imaginary) husband. She never married, and fell in love just once, with a dashing British army officer. She once wrote him a twenty-four-page letter that he never answered.

Nothing fazed her, even sliding down a hill and falling through someone's

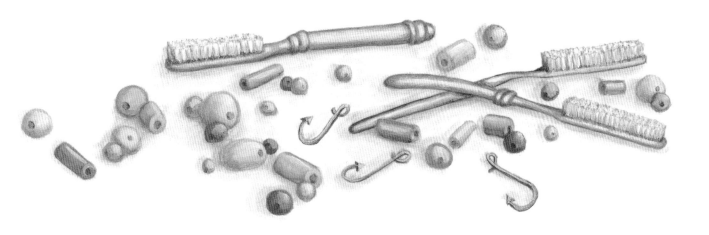

roof. She scared away a leopard by flinging a gourd of lime water at it, prodded huge hippos with her umbrella to move them from her path, and learned to deal with mosquitoes and bouts of malaria. She could wield a machete to hack her way through the forest. Her canoe was once surrounded by crocodiles as long as twenty-one feet; when one tried to get into her boat, she promptly beat it back with her paddle.

Kingsley enjoyed swamps more than social obligations; she was always reluctant to return to London between voyages. Visitors to her apartment there were greeted by a three-foot-high African idol, crusty with blood and studded with nails. She hated the "treadmill life" of the city, and its fast-moving conveniences (bicycles, taxis) gave her the "dazzles."

She admired traditional African beliefs as well as Islam. She described herself as a worshipper of the "great God of Science," and was not known to ever go to church. Going up against the Church of England, she criticized Christian missionaries, who she believed trivialized African traditions. She couldn't stand any European policies that took away the local culture, calling it a "murder."

A friend described Kingsley as combining "pure spontaneous mirth" with "profoundly deep seriousness." She always wore black, sometimes with a white cotton blouse, and was adamant about never wearing pants. She packed a revolver (but never used it) and a bowie knife. She smoked and drank wine, couldn't do without tea, and tended to lose weight on her diet of African fish stews, melons, and pumpkins. She wasn't shy about swearing and could take both God's and Allah's name in vain.

Although she once declared, "I believe that a woman has more deep-down endurance than a man," Kingsley did not support the right of women to vote. She claimed that suffragettes were "shrieking females," that she spent just as much time cooking as doing science, and that her father, like many men, had "had a perfect horror of highly educated women."

Yet this attitude didn't stop Kingsley from exploring Africa again and again, bringing back valuable information and specimens for natural history collections.

She wrote books full of witty descriptions and lectured to audiences as large as 1,700 people. Her strong sympathy for black Africans was novel at the time; it contradicted the stance of the mighty British Empire that its own citizens were superior.

Mary Kingsley had plans for many more trips and would have devoted the rest of her life to traveling. But she died of typhoid at age thirty-seven while nursing sick prisoners in South Africa, having explored for just seven years.

ONWARD

As an authority on African culture, Kingsley campaigned for just treatment and influenced how Europeans thought about Africa, a continent mostly unknown to them. After her death, organizations were formed in her honor to improve conditions for the native residents of British colonies.

Fishing was Kingsley's favorite way to relax in Africa, and she loved to collect specimens of previously unknown fish for the British Museum. Three were later named after her.

Her books, *Travels in West Africa* and *West African Studies,* were big bestsellers in her day and continue to be read. But Kingsley is not as well-known as male explorers of her time. She would have hated *A Woman Among Savages,* a 1950 biography of her, for its use of the word "savages" and its focus on her gender.

The Kind One

MATTHEW HENSON

Born in Nanjemoy, Maryland, 1866
Died in New York, New York, 1955

African American explorer who may have been the first person to reach the North Pole

Matthew Henson and Robert Peary shared many an unappetizing meal in the frozen land around the North Pole. But in the United States they wouldn't have even been allowed to eat together, as restaurants were segregated into "black" and "white" sections.

They met while Peary was shopping for a sun hat to wear as he explored Nicaragua. Henson, the store's clerk, had more experience exploring than Peary did; Henson had gone to sea as a cabin boy at age twelve and sailed all over the world. Impressed with his resourcefulness, Peary hired him as a personal assistant for his trip to Nicaragua, and later relied on him during his eighteen stressful years of exploring the Arctic. "I cannot get along without him," the elder explorer once said.

"Henson was altogether the most efficient man with Peary," said another member of the Arctic team. Henson built sleds, trained dog teams, constructed snow houses, and was the only one of the team who mastered the language of the local residents, the Inuit. The Inuit taught him their skills for survival in the harsh climate, like how to put moss inside his boots for protection against the deadly cold, and Henson in turn taught the other members of Peary's team.

The Inuit called him a name that meant "Matt, the Kind One" and told stories and sang songs about him. "I have come to love these people," Henson said, sharing their food and their sleeping quarters. He found that they tended to snore so loudly that a good night's sleep was impossible. His solution was to wake them up for a chat, then try to fall back asleep first. He claimed, "After that, their rhythmic snores will only tend to soothe and rest you."

Henson married twice in the States and had his only child with an Inuit woman. He read Dickens, Kipling, Peary's books, and the Bible, but said, "Mostly I had rougher things than reading to do." To head off frostbite, he danced to keep his blood circulating. Peary wasn't so lucky—most of his toes snapped off after an episode of bad frostbite. After this, Peary had to be carried everywhere, making Henson more indispensable than ever.

In 1909, Peary and Henson, along with four Inuit, became the first men to reach the North Pole. Peary, riding in a dogsled, sent Henson ahead as a scout. "I could see that my footprints were the first at the spot," Henson told a newspaper reporter later. The men planted the American flag: "A thrill of patriotism ran through me." Henson was immensely proud of his team's accomplishment: "There is no more beyond. . . . The geographical mind is at rest."

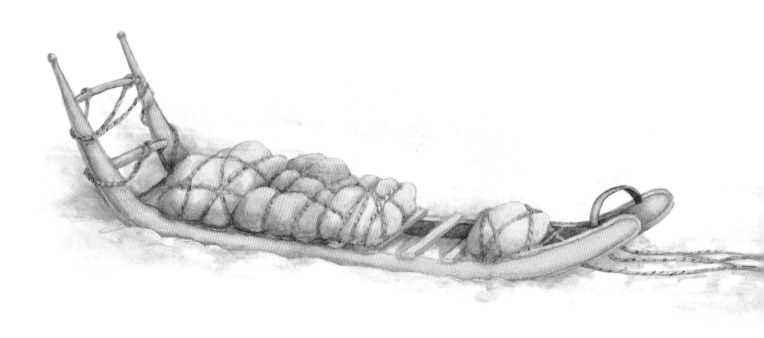

Peary wrote in his journal: "The Pole at last!!! The prize of three centuries. My dream and goal for twenty years. Mine at last!" Then he stopped speaking to Henson; he didn't even say goodbye after their North Pole triumph.

Henson was hurt and baffled. Over the years he wrote letters to Peary, but the only answer was a telegram forbidding Henson to use his photos of their trip in his lectures. Henson guessed that Peary had wanted to be the one to plant the flag, or was upset that he had to be carried the last two hundred miles while Henson had been able to walk.

Back at home, Henson received the same Congressional Medal as did all the North Pole team members and became the first black member of the prestigious Explorers Club. But Peary received the lion's share of the honors, plus a generous pension.

Henson spent most of the next thirty years as a government clerk in New York. He died of a stroke at age eighty-eight.

NAMING A NEW LAND AFTER "MOMMIE"

RICHARD E. BYRD

BORN IN WINCHESTER, VIRGINIA, 1888
DIED IN BOSTON, MASSACHUSETTS, 1957

American explorer of the North and South Poles

Richard Byrd was short and frail but fiercely dedicated to physical fitness. As a young gymnast, he invented a stunt that felt like flying, though he broke several bones doing it. By sixteen, reading every tome in his father's library, Byrd was forming a towering ambition to become an explorer.

While serving in the navy with distinction, he fell in love with flying airplanes, saying that "conquering the forces of wind and gravity had added to man's triumph over Nature." Byrd decided to be the first to fly over the North Pole. In a 1926 flight lasting fifteen and a half hours, he claimed to have made it. But many believe the first was Roald Amundsen, a Norwegian who flew a few days after Byrd. Three years later, Byrd and three companions made the first flight over the South Pole. This claim went undisputed, and Byrd became an international hero.

In five increasingly complex expeditions to the polar regions, he commanded thousands of men and dozens of planes, using the very latest technology to map the area. He brought along his fox terrier, Igloo, as well as medicine bottles full of cognac. He struggled to be a good leader, and headed off boredom and mutiny by organizing classes and forming clubs for his crews.

Back home, Byrd was honored with three ticker-tape parades and thousands of letters from young fans. But he also had enemies and claimed to receive many death threats. Some thought he was obsessed with one-upmanship, and that his real talent was not exploring but creating great publicity.

Byrd's most grueling feat came in Antarctica at age forty-five, when he chose to spend five months alone in a hut buried under ice. He manned a weather station and made important scientific observations at temperatures as low as seventy-six degrees below zero: "The cold seemed to shrivel my bones." He was planning to write, be creative, and stay sane with solitaire, music, *The Travels of Marco Polo,* and a fierce exercise routine. But he weakened, and one night went into a near-fatal panic. When he was finally rescued, Byrd was ailing from frostbite and carbon monoxide poisoning. Humiliated, he was in poor health for several years.

Funding his trips was always a burden. He went on speaking tours, begging the rich and famous to back him. Byrd found the stress of touring harder than exploring: "The most trying work I know. . . . It can well break the strongest man in a few months."

His wife, Marie, had been his childhood sweetheart; they had four children. Byrd kept in touch mostly by letter, since he was almost always away from home. "I have named a big new land after Mommie because Mommie is the sweetest, finest, and nicest and best person in the whole world," he wrote his young son after he named a new discovery Marie Byrd Land.

Byrd remained in love with flying, hoping that aviation would "become the world's strongest instrument for peace" by bringing people together and easing the spread of knowledge. He died in his sleep at age sixty-eight.

AUGUSTE AND JACQUES PICCARD

BORN IN BASEL, SWITZERLAND, 1884; DIED IN LAUSANNE, SWITZERLAND, 1962 (AUGUSTE)
BORN IN BRUSSELS, BELGIUM, 1922; DIED IN LA TOUR-DE-PEILZ, SWITZERLAND, 2008 (JACQUES)

Swiss explorers who flew higher and dove deeper than anyone

"There was nothing to cause us anxiety," Auguste Piccard insisted. "Neither my son nor I could believe in the possibility of a fatal accident." Their adventures were hair-raising (especially to their wives) but never deadly. Auguste and his son, Jacques, were not just daredevil explorers, but ultra-resourceful scientists.

Auguste, an esteemed professor of physics, wanted to study particles in the upper stratosphere. Could humans survive at that altitude? He began his exploring career by setting out to prove it, inventing a revolutionary lighter-than-air balloon that had features now common on airplanes, such as a pressurized cabin.

The headgear Auguste invented for his balloon flight never really caught on. The "aero-helmet" was a basket meant to offer protection in a crash, and could do triple duty as storage for instruments and a cushion to sit on. Even without the basket on his head, Auguste was always a sight to see: as skinny as a beanpole, with an unusually long neck, nearly blind without his thick glasses, wisps of hair flying every which way.

Auguste and a fellow scientist-adventurer made their historic ascent in 1931, reaching an altitude of nine miles above Earth. Before their safe return, they spent seventeen hours surrounded by an impossible shade of blue, encountering problems but quickly crafting solutions.

Auguste had opened the door to the Space Age. Watching the electrifying feat was a crowd that included his son, Jacques, then nine years old.

Always generous and kind, Auguste didn't gloat, but instead encouraged others to break his record: "It will be a fine day for me when other stratospheric balloons follow me and reach altitudes greater than I have."

Auguste and his wife, Marianne, his former student, lived in the Swiss Alps with Jacques and his four sisters. Auguste designed and built their large house. Its swimming pool was fed with water from a nearby spring, and music—piano, guitar, flute—was always in the air.

Auguste was actually more interested in going down than up. Ever since he was a child, he'd wanted to explore the sea: "The sea's surface is a frontier. . . . It is the ceiling of another world." How deep could one go? After his balloon feat, Auguste worked on an invention that would resist the pressure of the ocean depths: the bathy-scaphe, a word meaning "deep vessel." It helped that he was friends with the king and

queen of Belgium. Thanks to a casual mention of his "bathy" at a royal party, he got the financial support he needed.

But Auguste had trouble with the invention until Jacques, now grown, quit his work in economics and joined him as a collaborator. The two sent down several unmanned trial runs before Auguste descended in the bathyscaphe to prove that it worked. The cabin was dark—he lit up his face with a flashlight so scuba divers could see him inside, and played chess to pass the time.

Finally, in 1953, Auguste and Jacques launched a new bathyscaphe called *Trieste*, taking trips that plunged them ever deeper into the ocean. It was Auguste's dream come true—a record-breaking triumph.

But he was nearing seventy, and Marianne put her foot down: no more dangerous adventures. Jacques, hooked on exploring, carried on his father's work. His wife, Marie-Claude, with whom he had three children, gave her approval.

Jacques's manners were usually exquisite, but he sometimes got irritated when nonscientists interfered with his work; he considered their recommendations silly, useless, or dangerous. He was tall (six feet, seven inches) and a man of few words and limited sense of humor. His idea of a joke was to ask a fellow scientist if he was satisfied with his instruments; if the scientist said he was, then Jacques would place an essay in front of him that read, "A true scientist or engineer is never completely satisfied with his instruments."

Jacques's coup came in 1960. He and a navy lieutenant set a new record by descending almost seven miles down to the lowest known point on earth: the Mariana Trench in the Pacific Ocean near Guam. As he described the feat, "In the name of science and humanity, the *Trieste* took possession of the abyss, the last extreme on our earth that remained to be conquered." The men spent nine hours seated in the tiny cabin with no room to move; tall Jacques had to scrunch. They had fifteen chocolate bars with them, but ate sparingly in case they ended up trapped for a long time.

When they reached the bottom, his companion said, "We are at a depth where no one has yet been." Jacques silently nodded, and the two men shook hands. They had proved that humans could survive at this extreme depth.

Out their porthole, the "immense liquid curtain" parted to reveal tiny blue and green creatures glowing in the dark, and then something astonishing: "Slowly, very slowly, this fish—apparently of the sole family, about a foot long and half as wide—moved away from us, swimming half in the bottom ooze, and disappeared." Oceanographers had always debated whether fish could live so deep in the ocean, and this seemed to be proof.

After Auguste died of heart failure at seventy-eight, safely in his bed, Jacques kept adventuring—and so did the rest of the thrilling Piccard family.

Jacques's son Bertrand made the first round-the-world balloon flight in 1999, crediting his father for giving him "confidence in the face of the unknown."

Auguste's identical twin brother, Jean, and his wife, Jeannette, also made break-throughs in balloon exploration. Jeannette was technically the first woman in space when she floated more than ten miles over Lake Erie in 1934, and was later an adviser to NASA (the National Aeronautics and Space Administration). Their son Don was the first to cross the English Channel in a hot air balloon.

Jacques carried on exploring until his death at age eighty-six. He was passionate about protecting the planet, fighting especially for a ban on the dumping of nuclear waste at sea. He described Earth as a "small, self-sufficient capsule traveling in space. If we want it to continue its journey without mishap, we must keep it clean and livable."

ONWARD

Jacques Cousteau, the famous French underwater explorer, worked with the Piccards and expanded on their exploits. Cousteau developed diving gear that would allow explorers to dive deep and learn much, much more about the oceans.

Auguste, with his classic absent-minded-professor appearance, lives on as the inspiration for Professor Cuthbert Calculus in The Adventures of Tintin series of comics. The artist, Hergé, saw Auguste on the street and was awed by his "interminable neck." Auguste also inspired Gene Roddenberry, creator of *Star Trek,* in which Captain Jean-Luc Picard is the captain of the starship *Enterprise.*

It took fifty years for someone else to brave the Mariana Trench. In a 2012 voyage sponsored by *National Geographic,* Canadian filmmaker James Cameron became the first to do it alone. He descended to 35,756 feet, establishing a new world-record depth for a solo descent.

BLAST OFF!

SALLY RIDE

BORN IN LOS ANGELES, CALIFORNIA, 1951
DIED IN LA JOLLA, CALIFORNIA, 2012

Scientist and the first American woman to explore outer space

"It was the coolest thing around," Sally Ride said about President John F. Kennedy's 1960s goal to send men into space.

She followed all the developments, but "I never thought about becoming an astronaut." The idea seemed just too remote for this Southern California teenage girl (and women weren't even allowed to become astronauts until 1976). She was always outdoors swimming or playing baseball or football, and was so skilled at tennis that she almost turned professional.

Sally was also a big reader: all the Nancy Drew mysteries; the Danny Dunn chapter books, about a science detective; the sports section of the newspaper; Superman comics; *Mad* magazine; and *Scientific American,* which her parents subscribed to as a way of encouraging her obvious interest in science. Reserved, she hated being called on in class but always got good grades.

In college, Ride majored in physics as well as English (specializing in Shakespeare). One day an ad in the Stanford University student newspaper jumped out at her: the National Aeronautics and Space Administration was seeking scientists for a space shuttle mission that would test robots. She applied that very day—and ultimately so did eight thousand other people. NASA selected thirty-five, and Ride, a Ph.D. candidate, made the cut. She earned her doctorate in astrophysics and began her astronaut training the same year.

The training was stressful, but Ride was chosen partly because she was extremely physically fit and known for keeping her cool. She had to be tough in the nearly all-male culture of Johnson Space Center: though the female astronauts numbered six, there were only four women among the four thousand other employees. Someone who trained with her said, "Sally was one of the quickest wits and keenest pranksters in our class." She loved flying so much that on her own she earned a private pilot's license. She married a fellow astronaut, Steven Hawley, and flew herself to the wedding. They divorced five years later.

Ride never forgot she was part of a team, not the star, and was not out for publicity: "I did not come to NASA to make history." She was always polite, even when enduring sexist questions about being the first woman in space: Would she wear a bra or makeup in space? Would she cry if things went wrong? On TV she was asked to demonstrate the privacy curtain around the space shuttle's toilet. (The development of private bathrooms on the shuttle had influenced the decision to finally allow women to be astronauts.) Comedians joked that the upcoming flight would be delayed while Ride shopped for a purse to match her shoes.

How did she cope? "In many cases," she said, "I suggest taking the high road and have a little sense of humor and let things roll off your back."

In 1983, at age thirty-two, Sally Ride made history as the first American woman (and the youngest American) to explore space. After launching into orbit aboard the *Challenger,* her team soared 160 miles above Earth. During the six tense days of the mission, Ride helped develop a robotic arm to retrieve and release communications satellites, did experiments, and performed all her duties flawlessly.

In photos of her in the spaceship, she is always grinning, her curls floating around her. She liked the weightlessness of zero gravity, and joked about how one should eat a sandwich in space: fast, before it floated away. She exercised on a treadmill and savored the view: "The sparkling blue oceans and bright orange deserts are glorious against the blackness of space."

Ride was aware of her privileged vantage point: "It's a totally different perspective, and it makes you appreciate, actually, how fragile our existence is." Seeing the "really thin royal-blue line" of the Earth's atmosphere prompted serious thoughts about the future: "It's the only planet we've got, and you can see the effect of humanity when you look back at Earth from space."

But mostly the adventure was just plain exhilarating. When the shuttle finally landed safely, Ride told reporters, "I'm sure it was the most fun I'll ever have in my life."

She spent a total of 343 hours in space in her lifetime, serving on a second *Challenger* space mission. That time she traveled with a childhood friend, Kathryn Sullivan, who became the first American woman to walk in space.

Ride was in training for a third mission on a different spacecraft when the *Challenger* exploded after its launch. All seven astronauts aboard died. With space travel halted for two years, Ride served on the commission that investigated the cause of the shocking accident.

She became a professor of physics and developed her passion for encouraging young people, especially girls, to realize that "science is really cool stuff." She wrote seven science books for children and started her own company, Sally Ride Science, to foster science education. "It's no secret that I've been reluctant to use my name for things," she said. "I haven't written my memoirs or let the television movie be made about my life. But this is something I'm very willing to put my name behind."

She wanted girls to fall in love with science, mathematics, technology, and exploring, just as she had. She was well aware of the obstacles society traditionally put in the way of women who like science. "I never really thought of myself as a role model," Ride said. But once she became one, she did it with flair in spite of her shyness. "You can't be what you can't see," she declared.

But Ride worried about both girls and boys, pointing out that "our education system just isn't producing the skilled work force that we need to compete globally. . . . Fully eighty percent of the jobs in the future are going to require some background in science, math, and technology." All ordinary citizens, she said, need to be "scientifically literate" in order to compete in our complex world.

When Ride died of cancer at sixty-one, she left behind her partner of twenty-seven years.

The future of space exploration is cloudy, mainly because of its high cost in both money and human lives. But any manned missions yet to come will surely also be "womanned," thanks to Sally Ride.

ONWARD

Establishing a colony on Mars is one of the current goals in space exploration. Even if scientists knew how to get travelers back to Earth, the cost of a return journey would be prohibitive—so a trip to Mars would be one-way. "To boldly go where no one has gone before does not require coming home again," one supporter wrote. About one hundred thousand people have volunteered so far, including 76-year-old Valentina Tereshkova, the Russian woman who was launched into space nineteen years before Ride.

Ride loved to encourage young people to continue exploring space. Her most important tips were to start thinking as early as middle school about a career in space, and to study everything very hard, especially math and the area of science each student found most interesting. She liked to end every talk she ever gave to students with "Reach for the stars."

Mae Jemison, first African American woman in space, 1992

Alan Shepard, first American in space, 1961

Valentina Tereshkova, Russian, first woman to orbit Earth, 1963

Yuri Gagarin, Russian, first person to orbit Earth, 1961

John Glenn, first American to orbit Earth, 1962

More Pioneers
of Space
Exploration

Christa McAuliffe, American, first teacher in space, 1986

Neil Armstrong and Buzz Aldrin, American, first to walk on the moon, 1969

Guion Bluford, first African American man in space, 1983

For Further Reading

Bergreen, Laurence. *Columbus: The Four Voyages*. New York: Viking, 2011.

_____. *Marco Polo: From Venice to Xanadu*. New York: Knopf, 2008.

_____. *Over the Edge of the World: Magellan's Terrifying Circumnavigation of the Globe*. New York: Morrow, 2003.

Brown, Meredith Mason. *Frontiersman: Daniel Boone and the Making of America*. Baton Rouge: Louisiana State University Press, 2008.

Clark, Ella E., and Margot Edmonds. *Sacagawea of the Lewis and Clark Expedition*. Berkeley: University of California Press, 1983.

Danisi, Thomas C., and John C. Jackson. *Meriwether Lewis*. Amherst, New York: Prometheus Books, 2009.

Dreyer, Edward L. *Zheng He: China and the Oceans in the Early Ming Dynasty, 1405–1433*. New York: Pearson, 2007.

Foley, William E. *Wilderness Journey: The Life of William Clark*. Columbia, Missouri: University of Missouri Press, 2004.

Frank, Katherine. *A Voyager Out: The Life of Mary Kingsley*. Boston: Houghton Mifflin, 1986.

Henson, Matthew. *A Negro Explorer at the North Pole*. Montpelier, Vermont: Invisible Cities, 2001.

Hunter, Douglas. *Half Moon: Henry Hudson and the Voyage that Redrew the Map of the New World*. New York: Bloomsbury, 2009.

Kaye, Evelyn. *Amazing Traveler, Isabella Bird: The Biography of a Victorian Adventurer*. Boulder, Colorado: Blue Penguin, 1999.

Malkus, Alida. *Exploring the Sky and Sea: Auguste and Jacques Piccard*. Chicago, Kingston House, 1961.

McLynn, Frank. *Captain Cook: Master of the Seas*. New Haven: Yale University Press, 2011.

Rice, Edward. *Captain Sir Richard Francis Burton: A Biography*. New York: Da Capo, 1990.

Rose, Lisle A. *Explorer: The Life of Richard E. Byrd*. Columbia, Missouri: University of Missouri Press, 2008.

Wade, Linda R. *Sally Ride: The Story of the First American Female in Space*. Bear, Delaware: Mitchell Lane Publishers, 2003.

Waines, David. *The Odyssey of Ibn Battuta: Uncommon Tales of a Medieval Adventurer*. Chicago: University of Chicago Press, 2010.